Pocket ECGs

A Quick Information Guide

Bruce Shade, EMT-P, EMS-I, AAS

Higher Education

Boston   Burr Ridge, IL   Dubuque, IA   New York   San Francisco   St. Louis
Bangkok   Bogotá   Caracas   Kuala Lumpur   Lisbon   London   Madrid   Mexico City
Milan   Montreal   New Delhi   Santiago   Seoul   Singapore   Sydney   Taipei   Toronto

Higher Education

POCKET ECGS: A QUICK INFORMATION GUIDE

Published by McGraw-Hill, a business unit of The McGraw-Hill Companies, Inc., 1221 Avenue of the Americas, New York, NY 10020. Copyright © 2008 by The McGraw-Hill Companies, Inc. All rights reserved. No part of this publication may be reproduced or distributed in any form or by any means, or stored in a database or retrieval system, without the prior written consent of The McGraw-Hill Companies, Inc., including, but not limited to, in any network or other electronic storage or transmission, or broadcast for distance learning.

Some ancillaries, including electronic and print components, may not be available to customers outside the United States.

This book is printed on acid-free paper.

4 5 6 7 8 9 0 QLM 13 12 11

ISBN 978–0–07–351976–0
MHID 0–07–351976–6

Library of Congress Control Number: 2006931518

www.mhhe.com

Publisher, Career Education: *David T. Culverwell*
Senior Sponsoring Editor: *Claire Merrick*
Director of Development: *Kristine Tibbetts*
Developmental Editor: *Michelle L. Zeal*
Senior Marketing Manager: *Lisa Nicks*
Senior Project Manager: *Sheila M. Frank*
Senior Production Supervisor: *Kara Kudronowicz*
Senior Coordinator of Freelance Design: *Michelle D. Whitaker*
(USE) Cover Image: *© Tarhill Photos, Inc./CORBIS*
Compositor: *Electronic Publishing Services Inc., NYC*
Typeface: *11.5/12 Minion*
Printer: *Quad/Graphics, Leominster, MA*

Dedication

This book is dedicated to my wife Cheri, my daughter Katherine, and my son Christopher. Their love and support gave me the strength to carry this good idea from concept to a handy pocket guide.

Bruce Shade

Preface

This book, as its title implies, is meant to serve as a portable, easy to view, quick reference pocket guide. At your fingertips you have immediate access to the key characteristics associated with the various dysrhythmias and cardiac conditions. Essential (what you need to know) information is laid out in visually attractive color-coded pages making it easy to find the information for which you are looking. This allows you to quickly identify ECG tracings you see in the field or the clinical setting. It is also a useful tool in the classroom for quickly looking up key information. Small and compact, it can be easily carried in a pocket.

Chapter 1 provides a short introduction regarding the location of the heart and lead placement.

Chapter 2 briefly describes the nine-step process for interpreting the various waveforms and normal and abnormal features found on ECG tracings. It visually demonstrates how to calculate the heart rate, identify irregularities, and identify and measure the various waveforms, intervals and segments. Key values for each waveform, interval, and segment are listed. Chapters 3 through 7 lead you through dysrhythmias of the sinus node, the atria, the AV junction, the ventricles, and AV heart block. Characteristics for each dysrhythmia are listed in simple to view tables. Sample tracings include figures of the heart that illustrate where each dysrhythmia originates and how it occurs. This helps you understand the ECG dysrhythmia rather than just memorize strips. Chapter 8 introduces the concept of electrical axis. Chapters 9 and 10 introduce concepts important to 12-lead ECG interpretation and recognizing hypertrophy, bundle branch block, preexcitation and myocardial injury, ischemia, and infarction. Finally, Chapter 11 discusses other cardiac conditions and their effects on the ECG.

We hope this learning program is beneficial to both students and instructors. Greater understanding of ECG interpretation can only lead to better patient care everywhere.

Acknowledgments

I would first like to thank Lisa Nicks, Senior Marketing Manager, and the sales force at McGraw-Hill who came to Claire Merrick, our Sponsoring Editor and said the readers were clamoring for a simple to use tool to go along with our *Fast & Easy ECGs* textbook. Claire was quick to put the book on the front burner and get the project underway. I would like to thank Dave Culverwell, Publisher at McGraw-Hill. Dave embraced the idea of this book with great enthusiasm and lent his support and guidance. I would like to thank Michelle Zeal, the project's Developmental Editor. Michelle did a great job keeping things on track but yet did it in such a way that she didn't add a lot of stress to an already stressful process. Her hard work on the book shaped its wonderful look and style as well as helped ensure the accuracy of the content. This book, because of its dynamic, simplistic, visual approach, required significant expertise on the part of our production project manager, Sheila Frank. She helped condense a wealth of text and figures into a small compact pocket guide that maintains the warm, stimulating tapestry of its parent textbook, *Fast & Easy ECGs*.

Publisher's Acknowledgments

Rosana Darang, MD
Medical Professional Institute, Malden, MA

Carol J. Lundrigan, PhD, APRN, BC
North Carolina A&T State University, Greensboro, NC

Rita F. Waller
Augusta Technical College, Augusta, GA

Robert W. Emery
Philadelphia University, Philadelphia, PA

Gary R. Sharp, PA-C, M.P.H.
University of Oklahoma, Oklahoma City, OK

Lyndal M. Curry, MA, NREMT-P
University of South Alabama, Mobile, AL

The Electrocardiogram

1

What is in this chapter

- The ECG
  - The normal ECG
- The heart
- Conduction system
  - Waveform direction
- ECG paper

- ECG leads—I, II, III
- Augmented limb leads—aV_R, aV_L, and aV_F
- Precordial (chest) leads—V_1, V_2, V_3, V_4, V_5, and V_6
- Modified chest leads (MCL)

The ECG

- Identifies irregularities in heart rhythm.
- Reveals injury, death, or other physical changes in heart muscle.
- Used as an assessment and diagnostic tool in prehospital, hospital, and other clinical settings.
- Can provide continuous monitoring of heart's electrical activity.

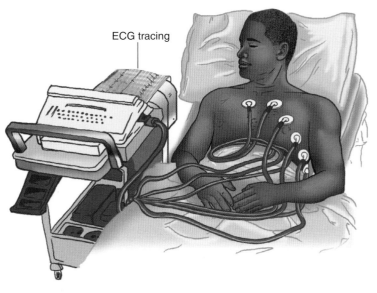

ECG tracing

Figure 1-1
The electrocardiograph is the device that detects, measures, and records the ECG.

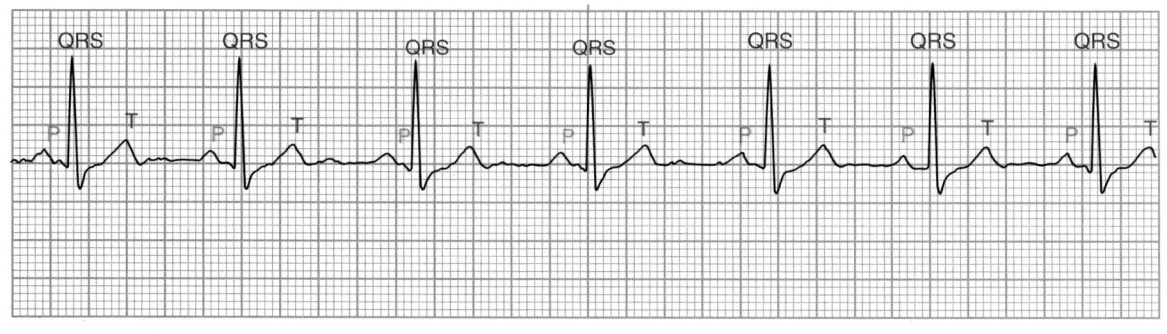

Figure 1-2
The electrocardiogram is the tracing or graphic representation of the heart's electrical activity.

The normal ECG

- Upright, round P waves occurring at regular intervals at a rate of 60 to 100 beats per minute.
- PR interval of normal duration (0.12 to 0.20 seconds) followed by a QRS complex of normal upright contour, duration (0.06 to 0.12 seconds), and configuration.
- Flat ST segment followed by an upright, slightly asymmetrical T wave.

The heart

- About the same size as its owner's closed fist.
- Located between the two lungs in mediastinum behind the sternum.
- Lies on the diaphragm in front of the trachea, esophagus, and thoracic vertebrae.
- About two thirds of it is situated in the left side of the chest cavity.

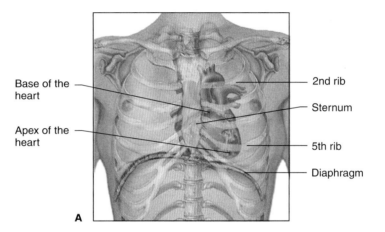

Base of the heart

Apex of the heart

2nd rib

Sternum

5th rib

Diaphragm

A

- Has a front-to-back (anterior-posterior) orientation.
  - Its base is directed posteriorly and slightly superiorly at the level of the second intercostal space.
  - Its apex is directed anteriorly and slightly inferiorly at the level of the fifth intercostal space in the left midclavicular line.
  - In this position the right ventricle is closer to the front of the left chest, while the left ventricle is closer to the left side of the chest.

Knowing the position and orientation of the heart will help you to understand why certain ECG waveforms appear as they do when the electrical impulse moves toward a positive or negative electrode.

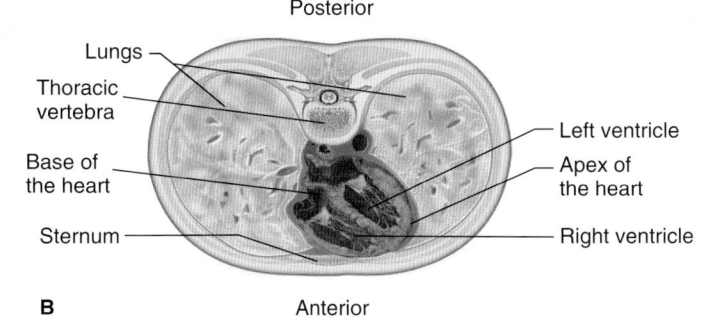

Figure 1-3

(a) Position of the heart in the chest.

(b) Cross section of the thorax at the level of the heart.

Conduction system

- Sinoatrial (SA) node initiates the heartbeat.
- Impulse then spreads across the right and left atrium.
- Atrioventricular (AV) node carries the impulse from the atria to the ventricles.
- From the AV node the impulse is carried through the bundle of His, which then divides into the right and left bundle branches.
- The right and left bundle branches spread across the ventricles and eventually terminate in the Purkinje fibers.

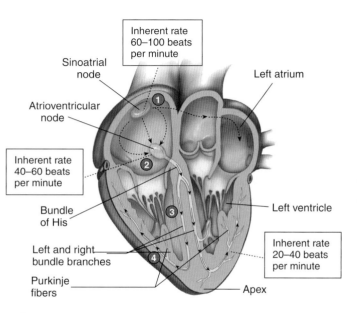

Figure 1-4
Electrical conductive system of the heart.

Waveform direction

- Direction an ECG waveform takes depends on whether electrical currents are traveling toward or away from a positive electrode.

Impulses traveling away from a positive electrode and/or toward a negative electrode will produce downward deflections.

Impulses traveling perpendicular to the positive electrode may produce a biphasic waveform (one that has both a positive and negative deflection).

Impulses traveling toward a positive electrode produce upward deflections.

Negative electrode

Positive electrode

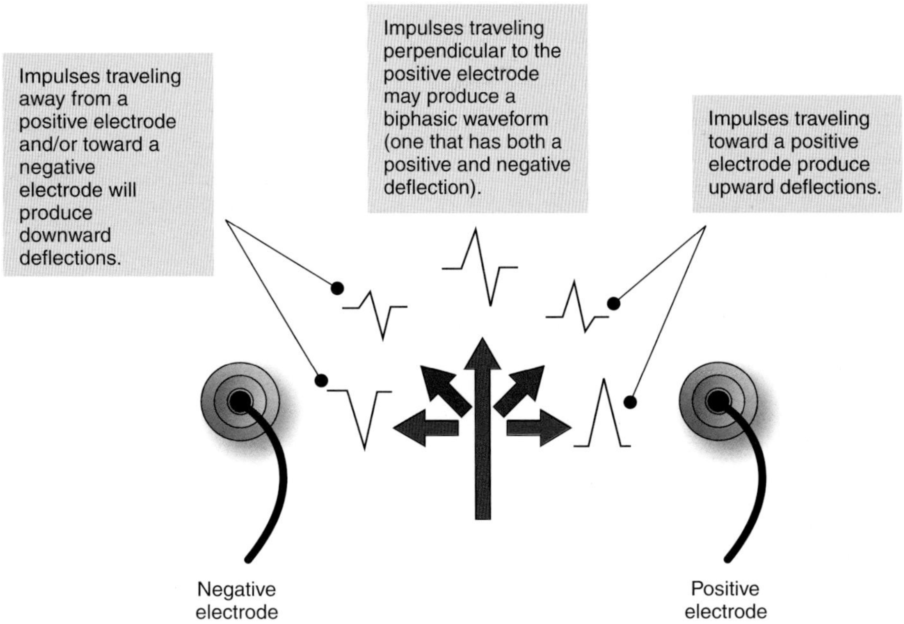

Figure 1-5
Direction of electrical impulses and waveforms.

ECG paper

- Grid layout on ECG paper consists of horizontal and vertical lines.

- Allows quick determination of duration and amplitude of waveforms, intervals, and segments.

- Vertical lines represent amplitude in electrical voltage (mV) or millimeters.

- Horizontal lines represent time.

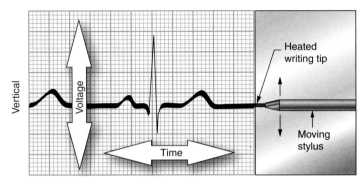

Figure 1-6
Recording the ECG.

- Each small square = 0.04 sec in duration and 0.1 mV in amplitude.
- Five small squares = one large box and 0.20 seconds in duration.
- Horizontal measurements determine heart rate.
- 15 large boxes = 3 seconds.
- 30 large boxes = 6 seconds.
- On the top or bottom of the printout there are often vertical markings to represent 1-, 3-, or 6-second intervals.

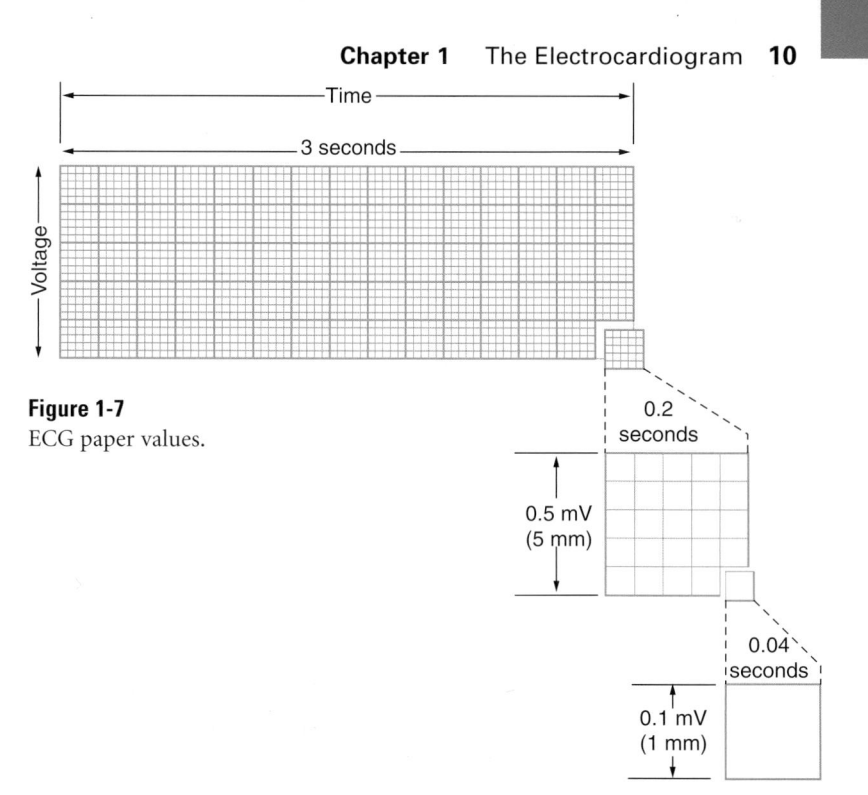

Figure 1-7
ECG paper values.

ECG leads— I, II, III

- Bipolar leads

Lead I

- Positive electrode—left arm (or under left clavicle).
- Negative electrode—right arm (or below right clavicle).
- Ground electrode—left leg (or left side of chest in midclavicular line just beneath last rib).
- Waveforms are positive.

To properly position the electrodes, use the lettering located on the top of the lead wire connector for each lead; LL stands for left leg, LA stands for left arm, and RA stands for right arm.

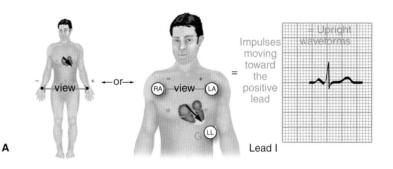

= Upright waveforms

Impulses moving toward the positive lead

A

Lead I

Lead II

- Positive electrode—left leg (or on left side of chest in midclavicular line just beneath last rib).
- Negative electrode—right arm (or below right clavicle).
- Ground electrode—left arm (or below left clavicle).
- Waveforms are positive.

Lead III

- Positive electrode—left leg (or left side of the chest in midclavicular line just beneath last rib).
- Negative electrode—left arm (or below left clavicle).
- Ground electrode—right arm (or below right clavicle).
- Waveforms are positive or biphasic.

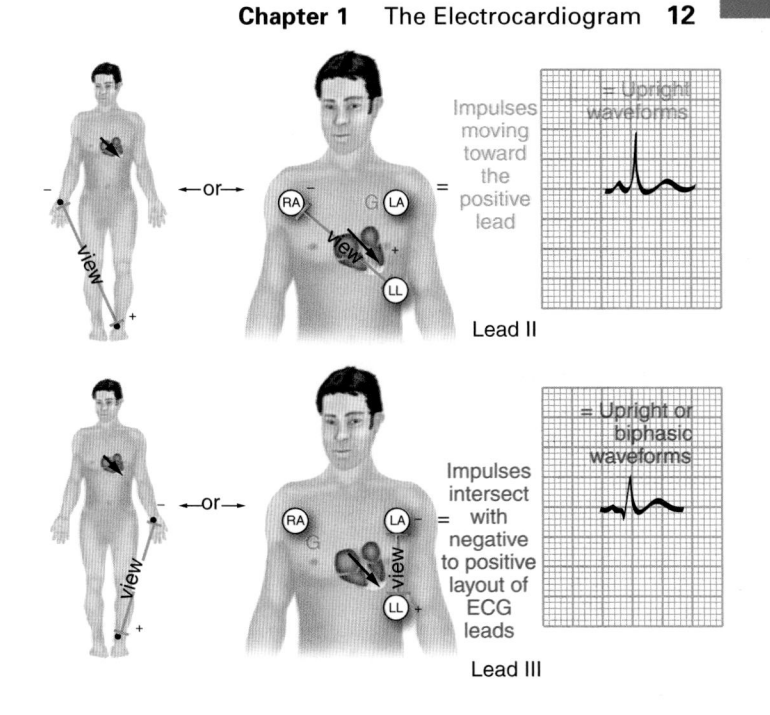

Figure 1-8 (a) Lead I. (b) Lead II. (c) Lead III.

Augmented limb leads—aV$_R$, aV$_L$, and aV$_F$

- Unipolar leads.
- Enhanced by ECG machine because waveforms produced by these leads are normally small.

Lead aV$_R$

- Positive electrode placed on right arm.
- Waveforms have negative deflection.
- Views base of the heart, primarily the atria.

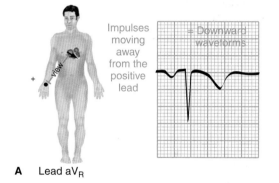

Impulses moving away from the positive lead = Downward waveforms

A   Lead aV$_R$

Lead aV$_L$

- Positive electrode placed on left arm.
- Waveforms have positive deflection.
- Views the lateral wall of the left ventricle.

Lead aV$_F$

- Positive electrode located on left leg.
- Waveforms have a positive deflection.
- Views the inferior wall of the left ventricle.

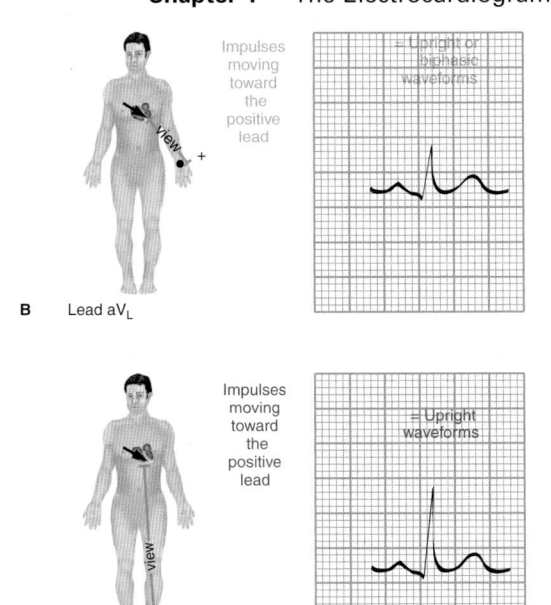

Figure 1-9 (a) Lead aV$_R$. (b) Lead aV$_L$. (c) Lead aV$_F$.

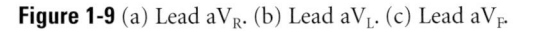

Precordial (chest) leads—V_1, V_2, V_3, V_4, V_5, and V_6

- Lead V_1 electrode is placed on the right side of the sternum in the fourth intercostal space.
- Lead V_2 is positioned on the left side of the sternum in the fourth intercostal space.
- Lead V_3 is located between leads V_2 and V_4.
- Lead V_4 is positioned at the fifth intercostal space at the midclavicular line.
- Lead V_5 is placed in the fifth intercostal space at the anterior axillary line.
- Lead V_6 is located level with V_4 at the midaxillary line.

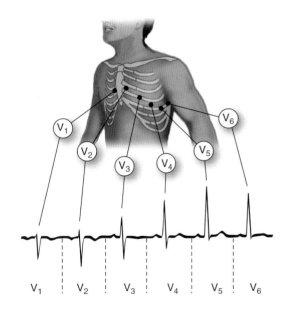

Figure 1-10 Precordial leads.

Modified chest leads (MCL)

- MCL$_1$ and MCL$_6$ provide continuous cardiac monitoring.
- For MCL$_1$, place the positive electrode in same position as precordial lead V$_1$ (fourth intercostal space to the right of the sternum).
- For MCL$_6$, place the positive electrode in same position as precordial lead V$_6$ (fifth intercostal space at the midaxillary line).

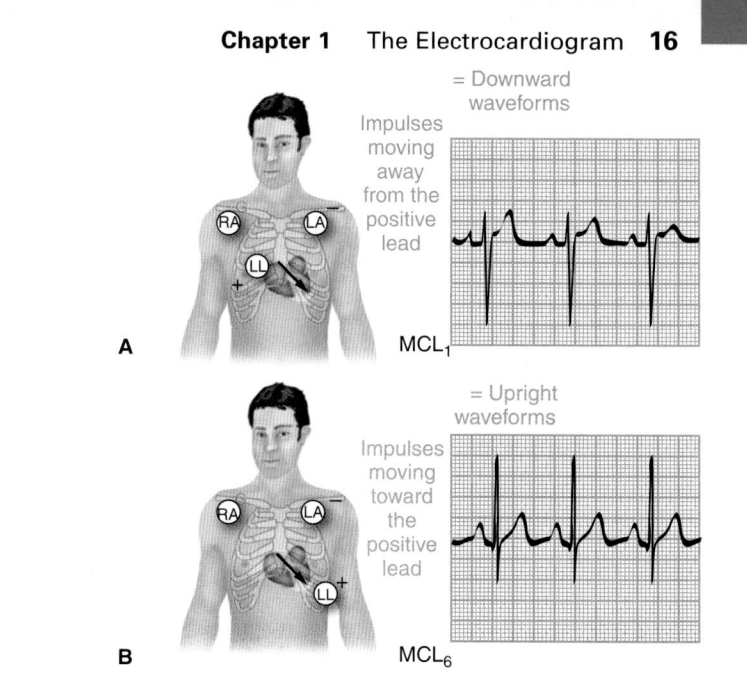

Figure 1-11 MCL leads. (a) MCL$_1$ and (b) MCL$_6$.

Analyzing the ECG

2

What is in this chapter

- Five-step (and nine-step) process
- Methods for determining the heart rate
- Dysrhythmias by heart rate
- Determining regularity
- Methods used to determine regularity
- ECG waveforms

Five-step (and nine-step) process

- The five-step process (and nine-step) is a logical and systematic process for analyzing ECG tracings

  1. Determine the rate. (Is it normal, fast, or slow?)

  2. Determine the regularity. (Is it regular or irregular?)

  3. Assess the P waves. (Is there a uniform P wave preceding each QRS complex?)

  4. Assess the QRS complexes. (Are the QRS complexes within normal limits? Do they appear normal?)

  5. Assess the PR intervals. (Are the PR intervals identifiable? Within normal limits? Constant in duration?)

Four more steps can be added to the five-step process making it a nine-step process.

  6. Assess the ST segment. (Is it a flat line? Is it elevated or depressed?)

  7. Assess the T waves. (Is it slightly asymmetrical? Is it of normal height? Is it oriented in the same direction as the preceding QRS complex?)

  8. Look for U waves. (Are they present?)

  9. Assess the QT interval. (Is it within normal limits?)

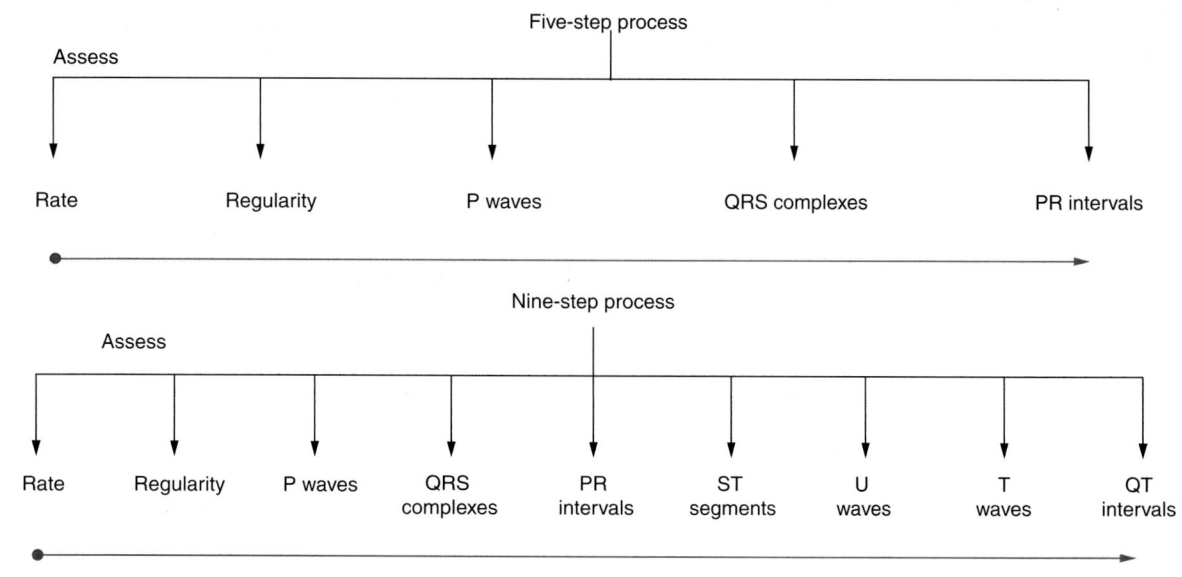

Figure 2-1 (a) The five-step process. (b) Nine-step process.

Methods for determining the heart rate

Using the 6-second × 10 method

- Multiply by 10 the number of QRS complexes (for the ventricular rate) and the P waves (for the atrial rate) found in a 6-second portion of ECG tracing. The rate in the ECG below is approximately 70 beats per minute.

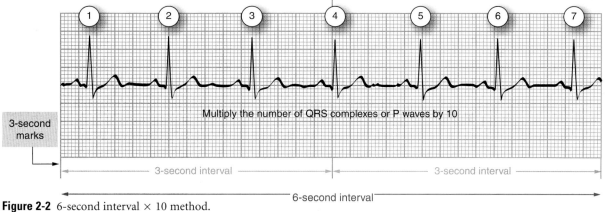

Figure 2-2 6-second interval × 10 method.

Using the 300, 150, 100, 75, 60, 50 method

- Begin by finding an R wave (or P wave) located on a bold line (the start point). Then find the next consecutive R wave. The bold line it falls on (or is closest to) is the end point and represents the heart rate.

- If the second R wave does not fall on a bold line the heart rate must be approximated.

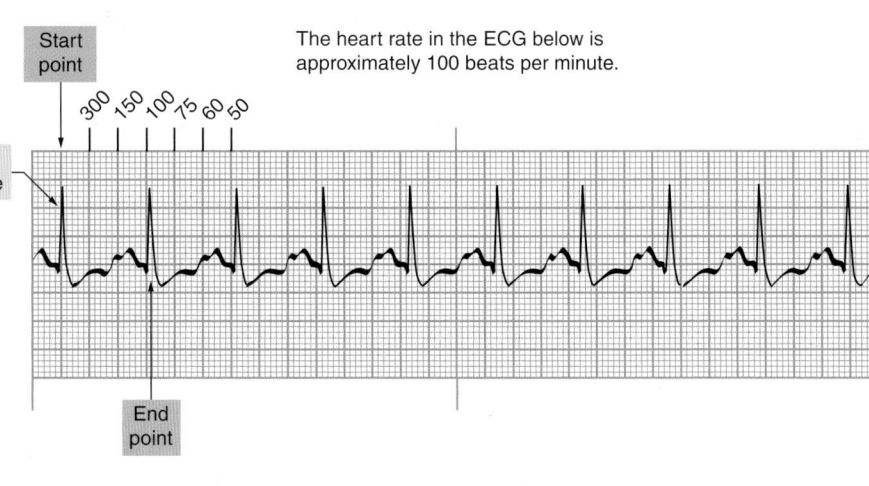

The heart rate in the ECG below is approximately 100 beats per minute.

Figure 2-3 300, 150, 100, 75, 60, 50 method.

Using the thin lines to determine the heart rate

- To more precisely determine the heart rate when the second R wave falls between two bold lines, you can use the identified values for each thin line.

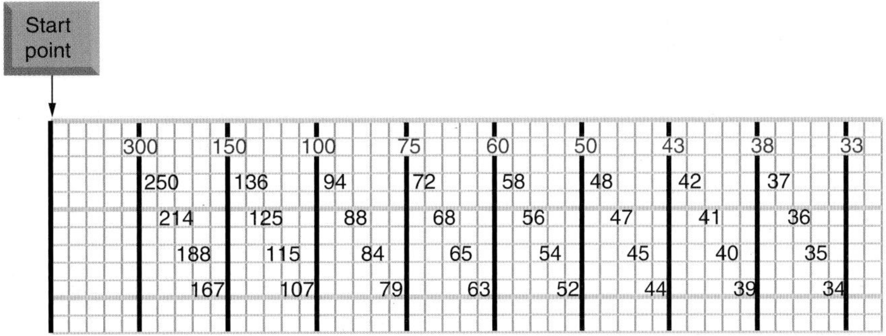

Figure 2-4 Identified values shown for each of the thin lines.

Using the 1500 method

- Begin by counting number of small squares between two consecutive R waves and divide 1500 by that number. Remember, this method cannot be used with irregular rhythms.

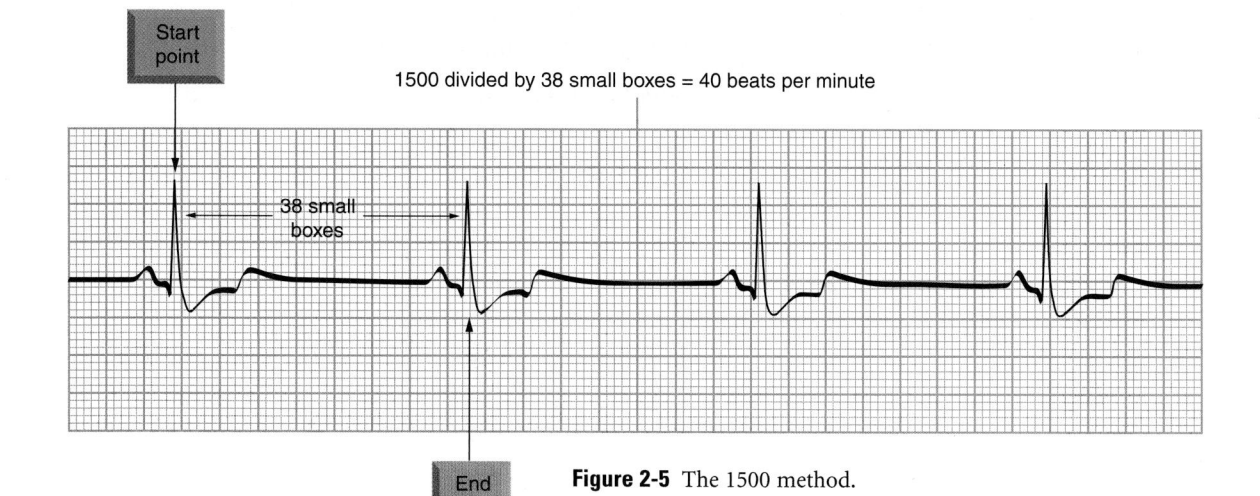

Figure 2-5 The 1500 method.

Dysrhythmias by heart rate

- Average adult has a heart rate of 60-100 beats per minute (BPM).
- Rates above 100 BPM or below 60 BPM are considered abnormal.
- A heart rate less than 60 BPM is called bradycardia.
  - It may or may not have an adverse affect on cardiac output.
  - In the extreme it can lead to severe reductions in cardiac output and eventually deteriorate into asystole (an absence of heart rhythm).
- A heart rate greater than 100 BPM is called tachycardia.
  - It has many causes and leads to increased myocardial oxygen consumption, which can adversely affect patients with coronary artery disease and other medical conditions.
  - Extremely fast rates can have an adverse affect on cardiac output.
  - Also, tachycardia that arises from the ventricles may lead to a chaotic quivering of the ventricles called ventricular fibrillation.

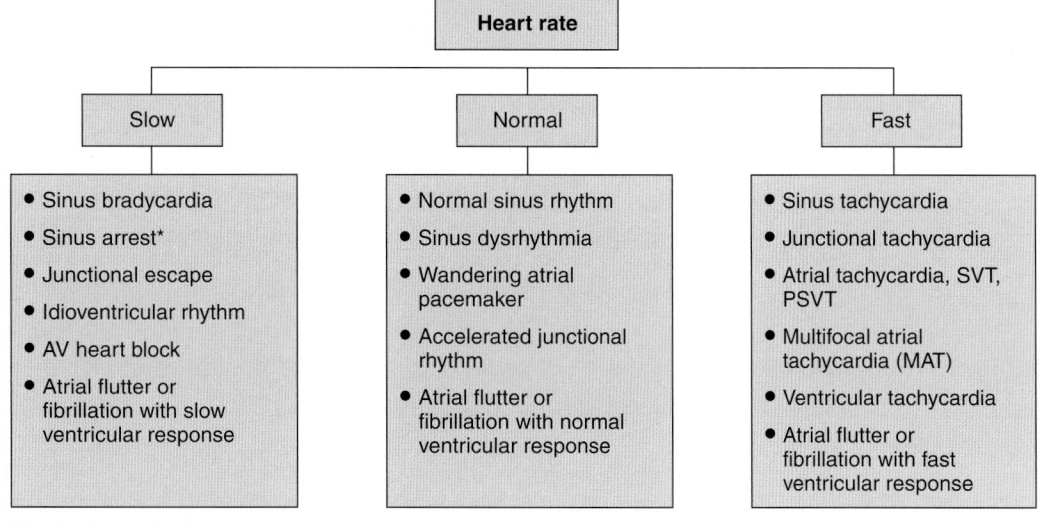

Figure 2-6 Heart rate algorithm.

Determining regularity

Equal R-R and P-P intervals

- Normally the heart beats in a regular, rhythmic fashion. If the distance of the R-R intervals and P-P intervals is the same, the rhythm is regular.

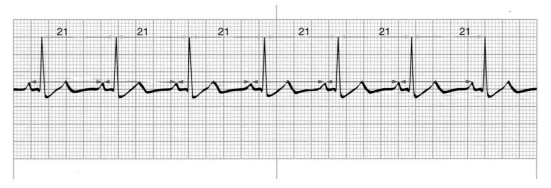

Figure 2-7 This rhythm is regular as each R-R and P-P interval is 21 small boxes apart.

Unequal R-R and P-P intervals

- If the distance differs, the rhythm is irregular.
- Irregular rhythms are considered abnormal.
- Use the R wave to measure the distance between QRS complexes as it is typically the tallest waveform of the QRS complex.
- Remember, an irregular rhythm is considered abnormal. A variety of conditions can produce irregularities of the heartbeat.

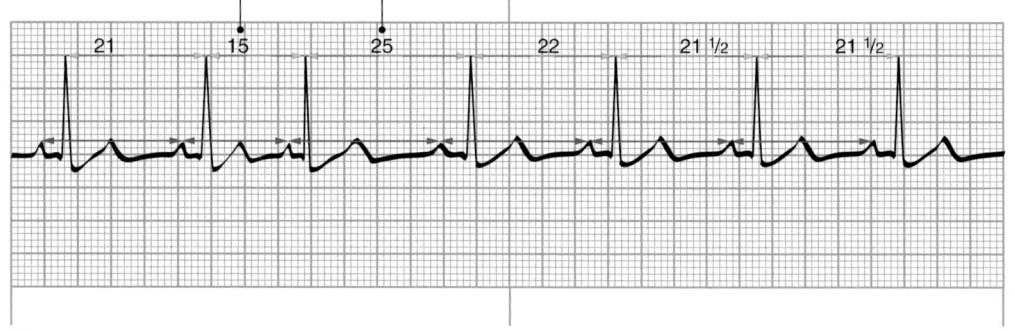

Figure 2-8 In this rhythm, the number of small boxes differs between some of the R-R and P-P intervals. For this reason it is considered irregular.

Methods used to determine regularity

Using calipers

- Place ECG tracing on a flat surface.
- Place one point of the caliper on a starting point, either the peak of an R wave or P wave.
- Open the calipers by pulling the other leg until the point is positioned on the next R wave or P wave.
- With the calipers open in that position, and keeping the point positioned over the second P wave or R wave, rotate the calipers across to the peak of the next consecutive (the third) P wave or R wave.

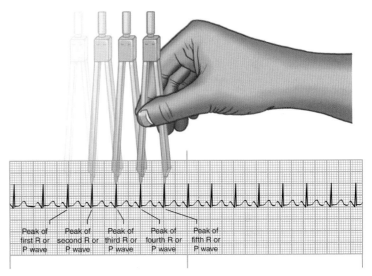

Figure 2-9 Use of calipers to identify regularity.

Using paper and pen

- Place the ECG tracing on a flat surface.
- Position the straight edge of a piece of paper above the ECG tracing so that the intervals are still visible.
- Identify a starting point, the peak of an R wave or P wave, and place a mark on the paper in the corresponding position above it.
- Find the peak of the next consecutive R wave or P wave, and place a mark on the paper in the corresponding position above it.
- Move the paper across the ECG tracing, aligning the two marks with succeeding R-R intervals or P-P intervals.

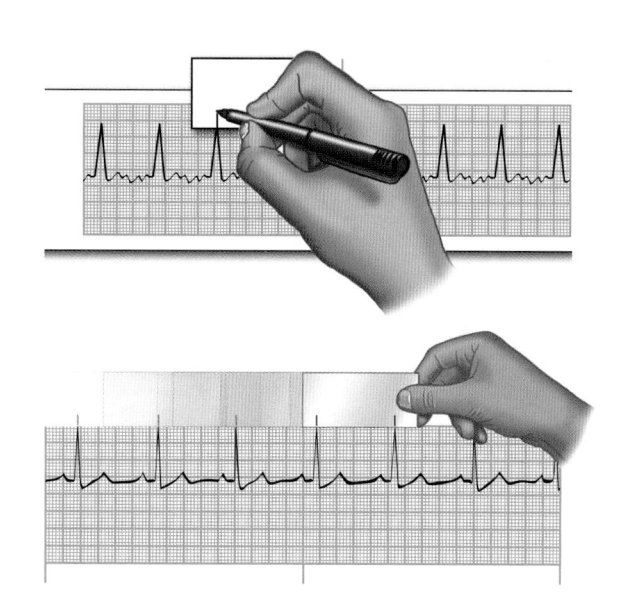

Figure 2-10 Use of paper and pen to identify regularity.

Counting the small squares between each R-R interval

- Count the number of small squares between the peaks of two consecutive R waves (or P waves) and then compare that to the other R-R (or P-P) intervals to reveal regularity.

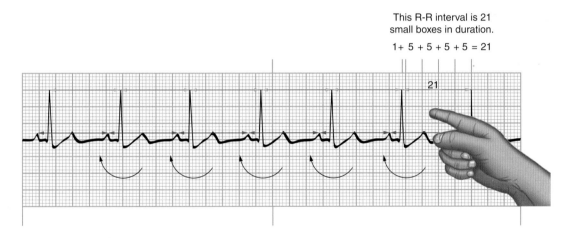

This R-R interval is 21 small boxes in duration.

1+ 5 + 5 + 5 + 5 = 21

Figure 2-11 Counting the number of small squares to identify regularity.

Types of irregularity

- Irregularity can be categorized as:
  - occasionally irregular or very irregular.
  - slightly irregular.
  - sudden acceleration in the heart rate.
  - patterned irregularly.
  - irregularly (totally) irregular.
  - variable conduction ratio.
- Each type of irregularity is associated with certain dysrhythmias. Knowing which irregularity is associated with which dysrhythmias makes it easier to later interpret a given ECG tracing.

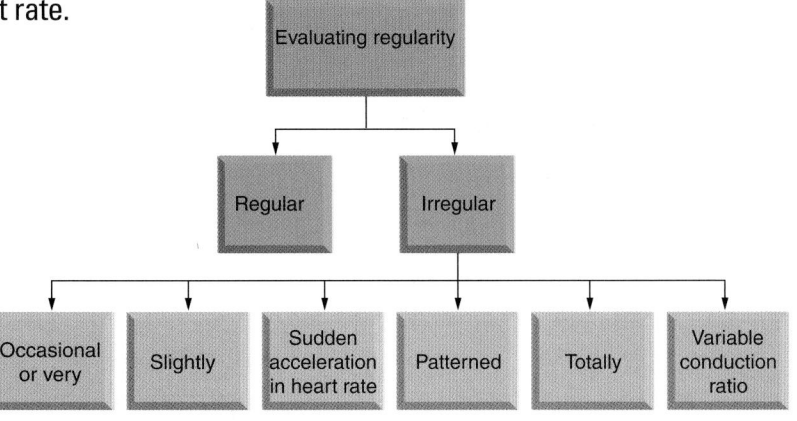

Figure 2-12 Algorithm for regular and irregular rhythms.

Occasionally irregular

- The dysrhythmia is mostly regular but from time to time you see an area of irregularity.

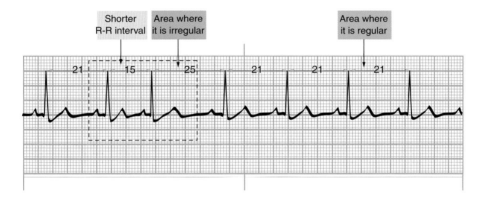

Figure 2-13 An occasionally irregular rhythm.

Frequently irregular

- A very irregular dysrhythmia has many areas of irregularity.

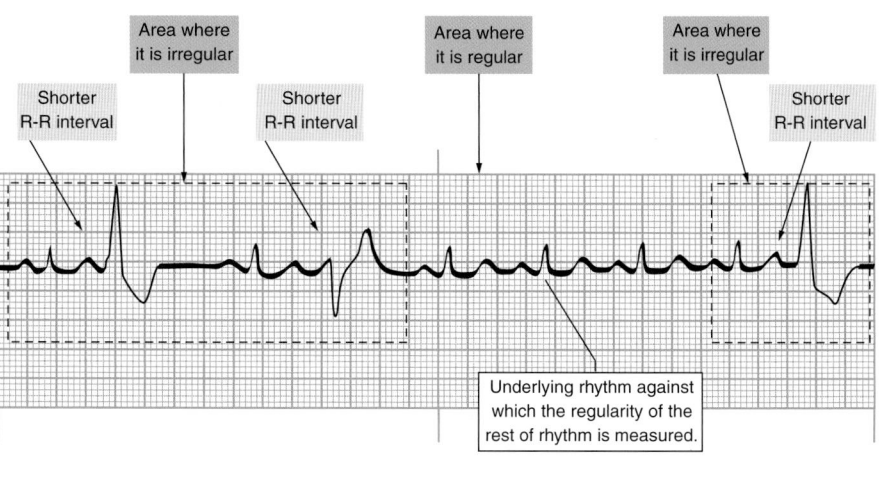

Figure 2-14 A frequently irregular rhythm.

Slightly irregular

- Rhythm appears to change only slightly with the P-P intervals and R-R intervals varying somewhat.

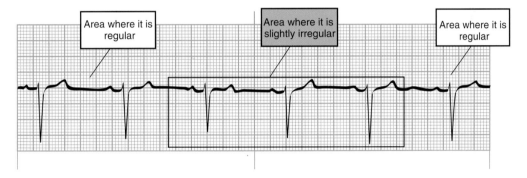

Figure 2-15 A slightly irregular rhythm.

Paroxsymally irregular

- A normal rate suddenly accelerates to a rapid rate producing an irregularity in the rhythm.

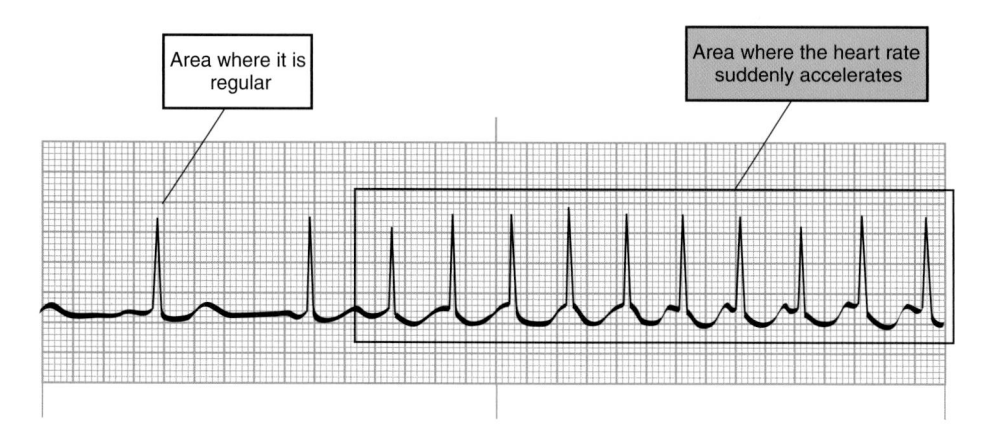

Area where it is regular

Area where the heart rate suddenly accelerates

Figure 2-16 A paroxsymally irregular rhythm.

Patterned irregularity

- The irregularity repeats in a cyclic fashion.

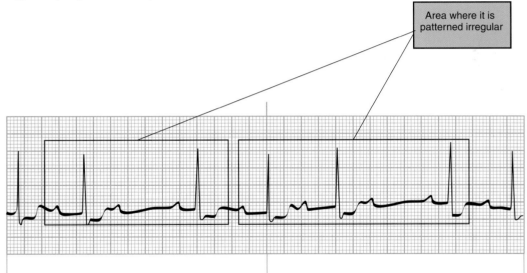

Area where it is patterned irregular

Figure 2-17 A patterned irregular rhythm.

Irregular irregularity

- No consistency to the irregularity.

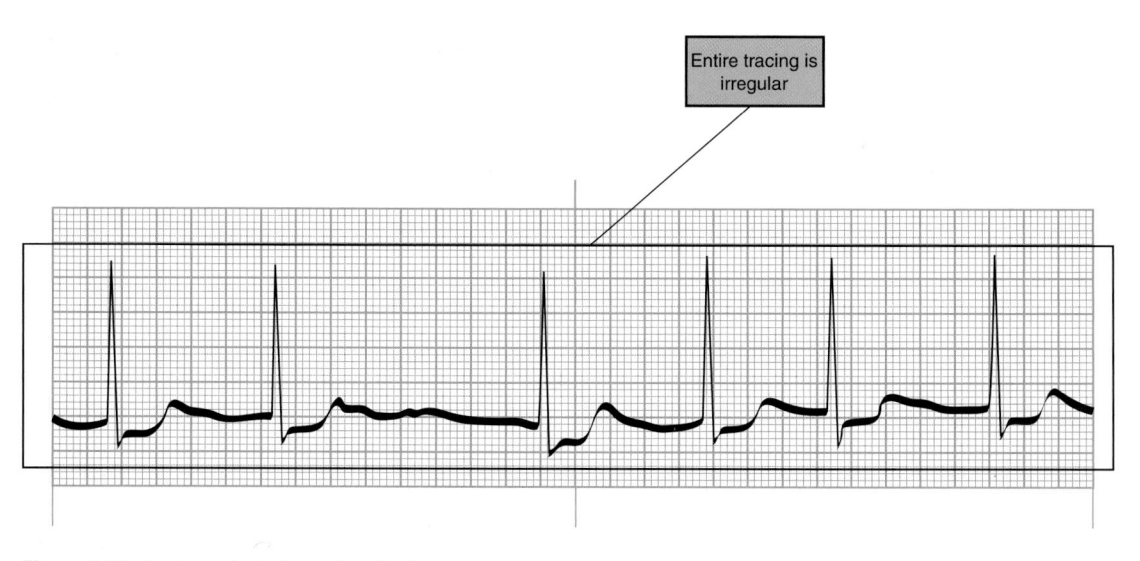

Entire tracing is
irregular

Figure 2-18 An irregularly irregular rhythm.

Variable irregularity

- The number of impulses reaching the ventricles changes, producing an irregularity.

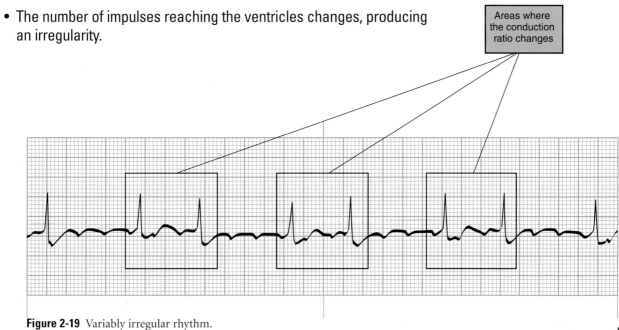

Areas where the conduction ratio changes

Figure 2-19 Variably irregular rhythm.

Irregularity algorithm

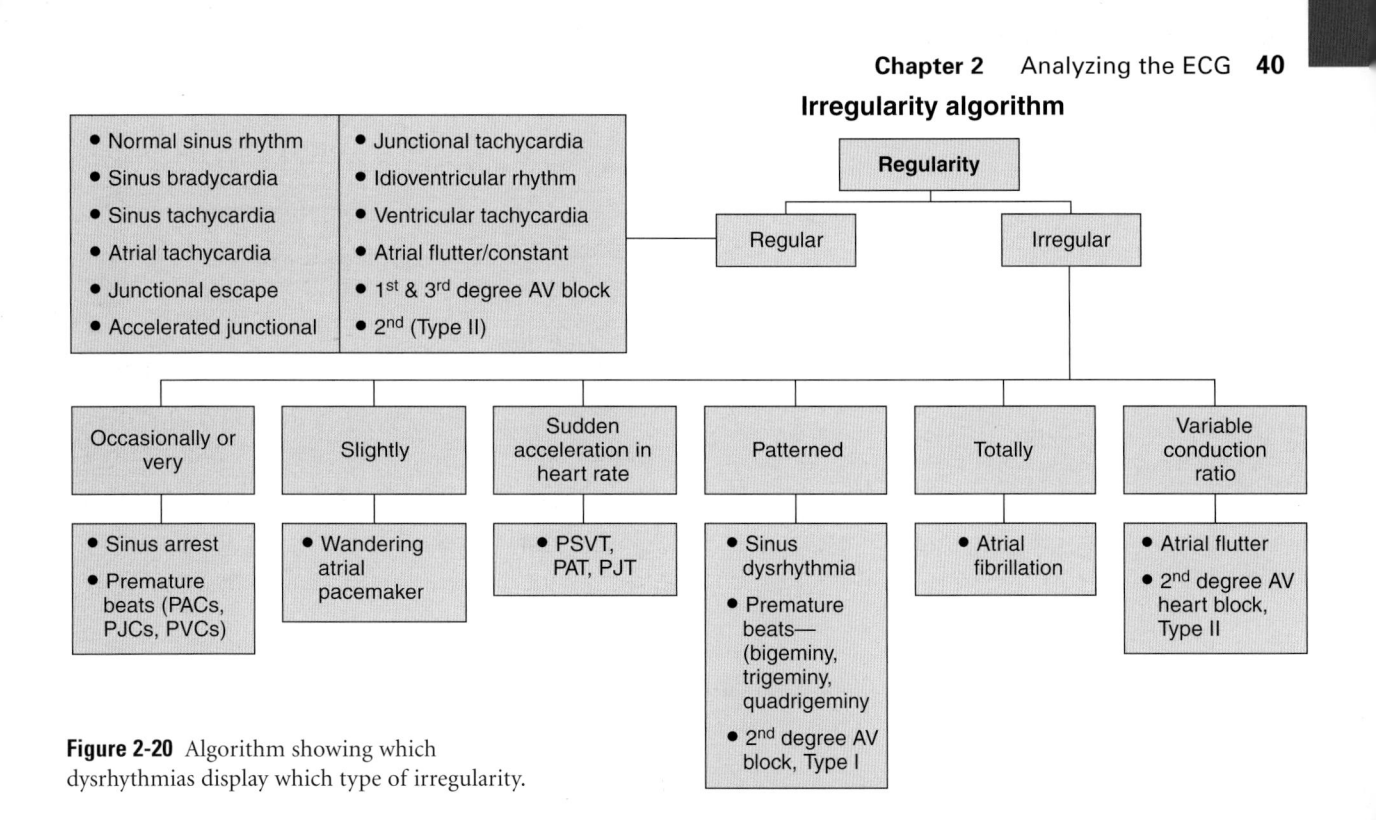

- Normal sinus rhythm
- Sinus bradycardia
- Sinus tachycardia
- Atrial tachycardia
- Junctional escape
- Accelerated junctional

- Junctional tachycardia
- Idioventricular rhythm
- Ventricular tachycardia
- Atrial flutter/constant
- 1st & 3rd degree AV block
- 2nd (Type II)

Regularity

Regular | Irregular

Occasionally or very | Slightly | Sudden acceleration in heart rate | Patterned | Totally | Variable conduction ratio

- Sinus arrest
- Premature beats (PACs, PJCs, PVCs)

- Wandering atrial pacemaker

- PSVT, PAT, PJT

- Sinus dysrhythmia
- Premature beats— (bigeminy, trigeminy, quadrigeminy
- 2nd degree AV block, Type I

- Atrial fibrillation

- Atrial flutter
- 2nd degree AV heart block, Type II

Figure 2-20 Algorithm showing which dysrhythmias display which type of irregularity.

ECG waveforms

P wave

- Begins with its movement away from the baseline and ends in its return to the baseline.
- Characteristically round and slightly asymmetrical.
- There should be one P wave preceding each QRS complex.
- In leads I, II, aV$_F$, and V$_2$ through V$_6$, its deflection is characteristically upright or positive.
- In leads III, aV$_L$, and V$_1$, the P wave is usually upright but may be negative or biphasic (both positive and negative).
- In lead aV$_R$, the P wave is negative or inverted.

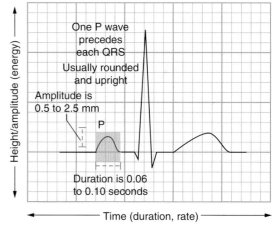

Figure 2-21 P wave.

QRS complex

- Follows PR segment and consists of:
  - ○ **Q wave**—first negative deflection following PR segment. It is always negative. In some cases it is absent. The amplitude is normally less than 25% of the amplitude of the R wave in that lead.
  - ○ **R wave**—first positive triangular deflection following Q wave or PR segment.
  - ○ **S wave**—first negative deflection that extends below the baseline in the QRS complex following the R wave.

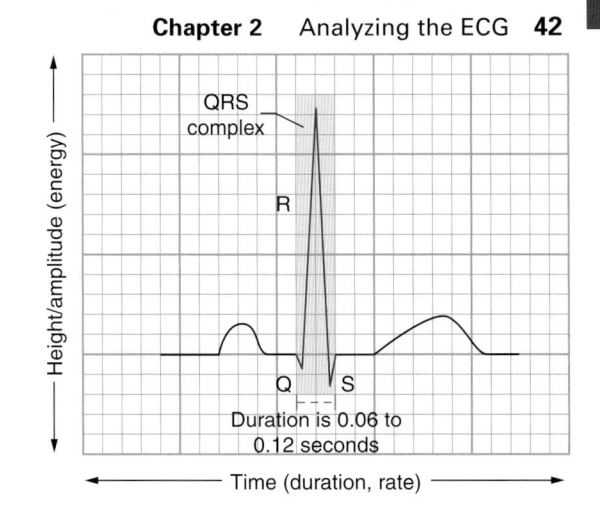

Figure 2-22 QRS complex.

- In leads I, II, III, aV$_L$, aV$_F$ and V$_4$ to V$_6$, the deflection of the QRS complex is characteristically positive or upright.

- In leads aV$_R$ and V$_1$ to V$_3$, the QRS complex is usually negative or inverted.

- In leads III and V$_2$ to V$_4$ the QRS complex may also be biphasic.

Differing forms of QRS complexes

- QRS complexes can consist of positive (upright) deflections called R waves and negative (inverted) deflections called Q and S waves: all three waves are not always seen.

- If the R wave is absent, complex is called a QS complex. Likewise, if the Q wave is absent, complex is called an RS complex.

- Waveforms of normal or greater than normal amplitude are denoted with a large case letter, whereas waveforms less than 5 mm amplitude are denoted with a small case letter (e.g., "q," "r," "s").

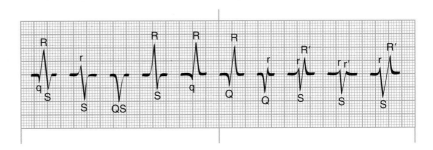

Figure 2-23 Common QRS complexes.

Measuring the QRS complex

- First identify the QRS complex with the longest duration and most distinct beginning and ending.
- Start by finding the beginning of the QRS complex.
  - This is the point where the first wave of the complex (where either the Q or R wave) begins to deviate from the baseline.
- Then measure to the point where the last wave of the complex transitions into the ST segment (referred to as the J point).
  - Typically, it is where the S wave or R wave (in the absence of an S wave) begins to level out (flatten) at, above, or below the baseline.
  - This is considered the end of the QRS complex.

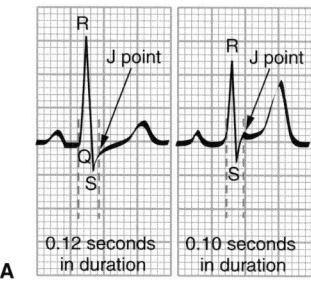

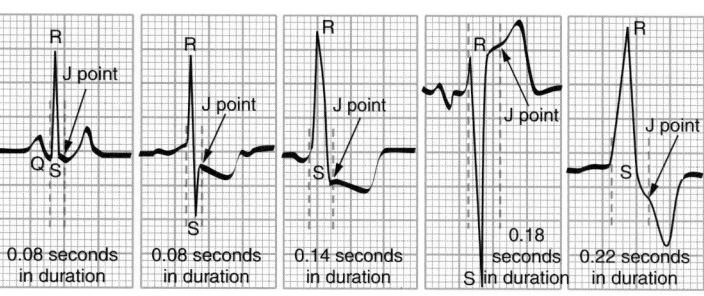

Figure 2-24 Measuring the QRS complex. (a) These two QRS complexes have easy to see J points. (b) These QRS complexes have less defined transitions making measurement of the QRS complex more challenging.

PR interval

- Extends from the beginning of the P wave to the beginning of the Q wave or R wave.
- Consists of a P wave and a flat (isoelectric) line.
- It is normally constant for each impulse conducted from the atria to the ventricles.
- The PR segment is the isoelectric line that extends from the end of the P wave to the beginning of the Q wave or R wave.

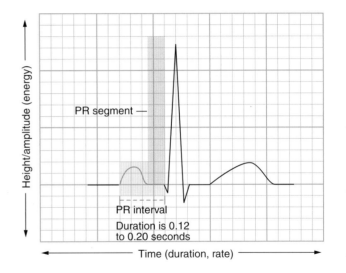

Figure 2-25 PR interval.

Measuring the PR interval

- To measure the width (duration) of a PR interval, first identify the interval with the longest duration and the most distinct beginning and ending.

- Start by finding the beginning of the interval. This is the point where the P wave begins to transition from the isoelectric line.

- Then measure to the point where the isoelectric line (following the P wave) transitions into the Q or R wave (in the absence of an S wave).

- This is considered the end of the PR interval.

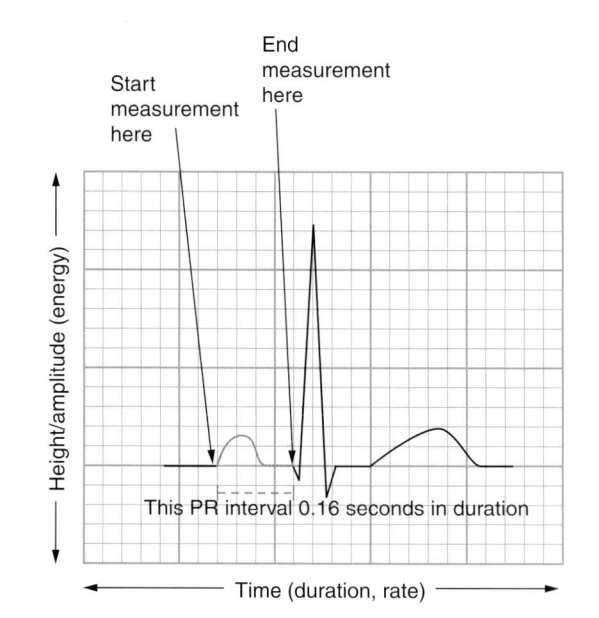

Figure 2-26 Measuring PR intervals.

ST segment

- The line that follows the QRS complex and connects it to the T wave.

- Begins at the isoelectric line extending from the S wave until it gradually curves upward to the T wave.

- Under normal circumstances, it appears as a flat line (neither positive nor negative), although it may vary by 0.5 to 1.0 mm in some precordial leads.

- The point that marks the end of the QRS and the beginning of the ST segment is known as the J point.

- The PR segment is used as the baseline from which to evaluate the degree of displacement of the ST segment from the isoelectric line.

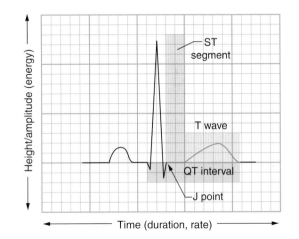

Figure 2-27 ST segment, T wave, and QT interval.

- Measure at a point 0.04 seconds (one small box) after the J point. The ST segment is considered elevated if it is above the baseline and considered depressed if it is below it.

T wave

- Larger, slightly asymmetrical waveform that follows the ST segment.
- Peak is closer to the end than the beginning, and the first half has a more gradual slope than the second half.
- Normally not more than 5 mm in height in the limb leads or 10 mm in any precordial lead.
- Normally oriented in the same direction as the preceding QRS complex.
- Normally positive in leads I, II, and V_2 to V_6 and negative in lead aV_R. They are also positive in aV_L and aV_F but may be negative if the QRS complex is less that 6 mm in height. In leads III and V_1, the T wave may be positive or negative.

QT interval

- Distance from onset of QRS complex until end of T wave.
- Measures time of ventricular depolarization and repolarization.
- Normal duration of 0.36 to 0.44 seconds.

U wave

- Small upright (except in lead aV_L) waveform sometimes seen following the T wave, but before the next P wave.

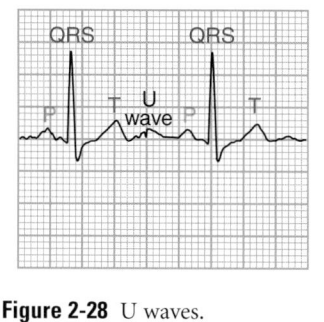

Figure 2-28 U waves.

Abnormal P waves

- P waves seen with impulses that originate in the SA node but travel through altered or damaged atria (or atrial conduction pathways) appear tall and rounded or peaked, notched, wide and notched or biphasic.

- P waves appear different than sinus P waves when the impulse arises from the atria instead of the sinus node.

- Sawtooth appearing waveforms (flutter waves) occur when an ectopic site in the atria fires rapidly.

- A chaotic-looking baseline (no discernible P waves) occurs when many ectopic atrial sites rapidly fire.

- P waves are inverted, absent, or follow the QRS complex when the impulse arises from the left atria, low in the right atria, or in the AV junction.

- More P waves than QRS complexes occur when impulses arise from the SA node, but do not all reach the ventricles due to a blockage.

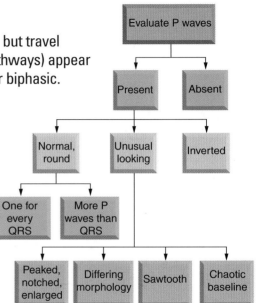

Figure 2-29 Algorithm for normal and abnormal P waves.

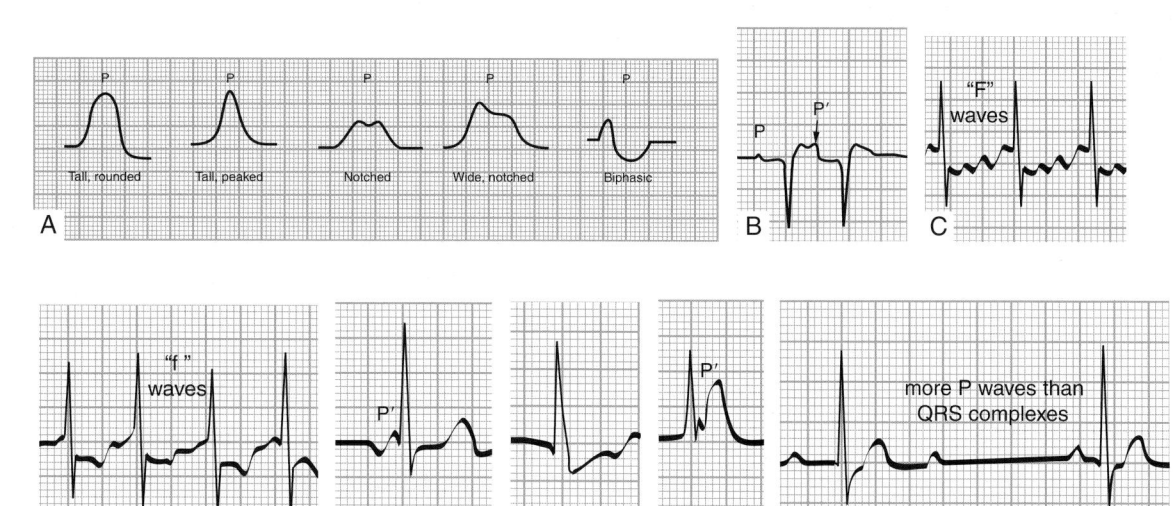

Figure 2-30 Types of waveforms: (a) abnormal sinus P waves, (b) atrial P wave associated with a PAC, (c) flutter waves, (d) no discernible P waves, (e) inverted P wave, (f) absent P wave, (g) P wave that follows QRS, and (h) P waves that are not all followed by a QRS complex.

Abnormal QRS complexes

- Abnormally tall due to ventricular hypertrophy or abnormally small due to obesity, hyperthyroidism, or pleural effusion.
- Slurred (delta wave) due to ventricular preexcitation.
- Vary from being only slightly abnormal to extremely wide and notched due to bundle branch block, intraventricular conduction disturbance, or aberrant ventricular conduction.
- Wide due to ventricular pacing by a cardiac pacemaker.
- Wide and bizarre looking due to electrical impulses originating from an ectopic or escape pacemaker site in the ventricles.

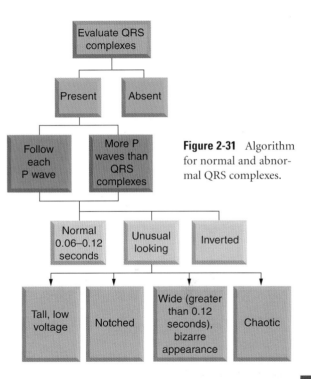

Figure 2-31 Algorithm for normal and abnormal QRS complexes.

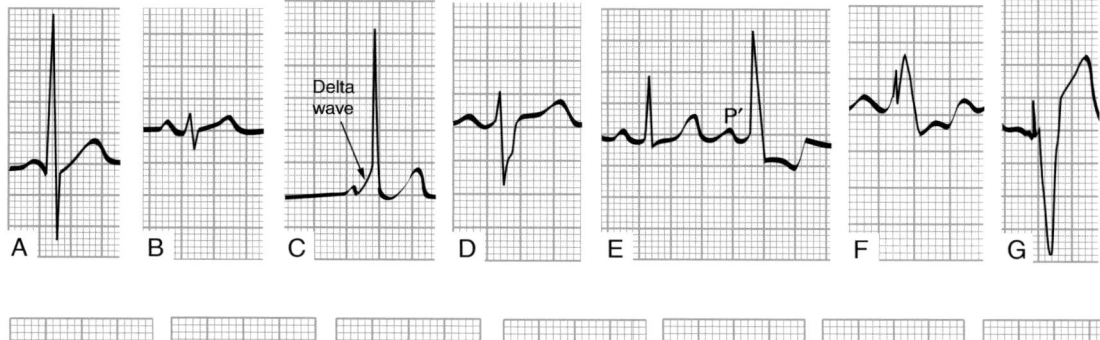

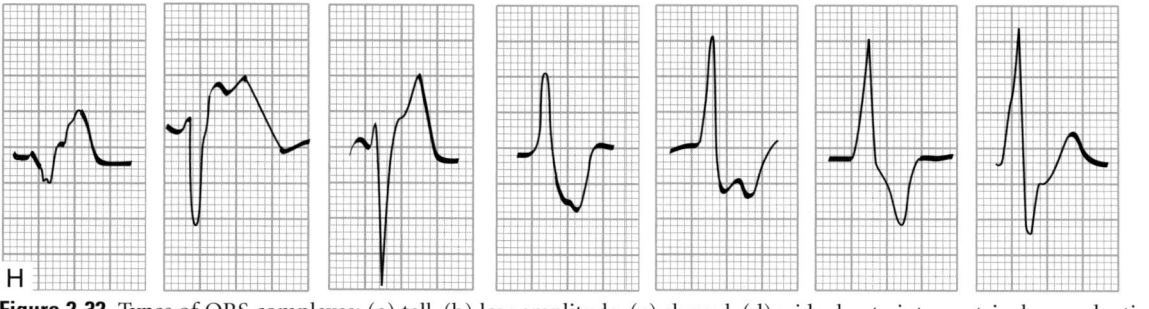

Figure 2-32 Types of QRS complexes: (a) tall, (b) low amplitude, (c) slurred, (d) wide due to intraventricular conduction defect, (e) wide due to aberrant conduction, (f) wide due to bundle branch block, (g) wide due to ventricular cardiac pacemaker, and (h) various wide and bizarre complexes due to ventricular origin.

Abnormal PR intervals

- Abnormally short or absent due to impulse arising from low in the atria or in the AV junction.
- Abnormally short due to ventricular preexcitation.
- Absent due to ectopic site in the atria firing rapidly or many sites in the atria firing chaotically.
- Absent due to impulse arising from the ventricles.
- Longer than normal due to a delay in AV conduction.
- Vary due to changing atrial pacemaker site.
- Progressively longer due to a weakened AV node that fatigues more and more with each conducted impulse until finally it is so tired that it fails to conduct an impulse through to the ventricles.
- Absent due to the P waves having no relationship to the QRS complexes.

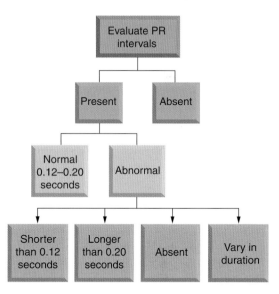

Figure 2-33 Algorithm for normal and abnormal PR intervals.

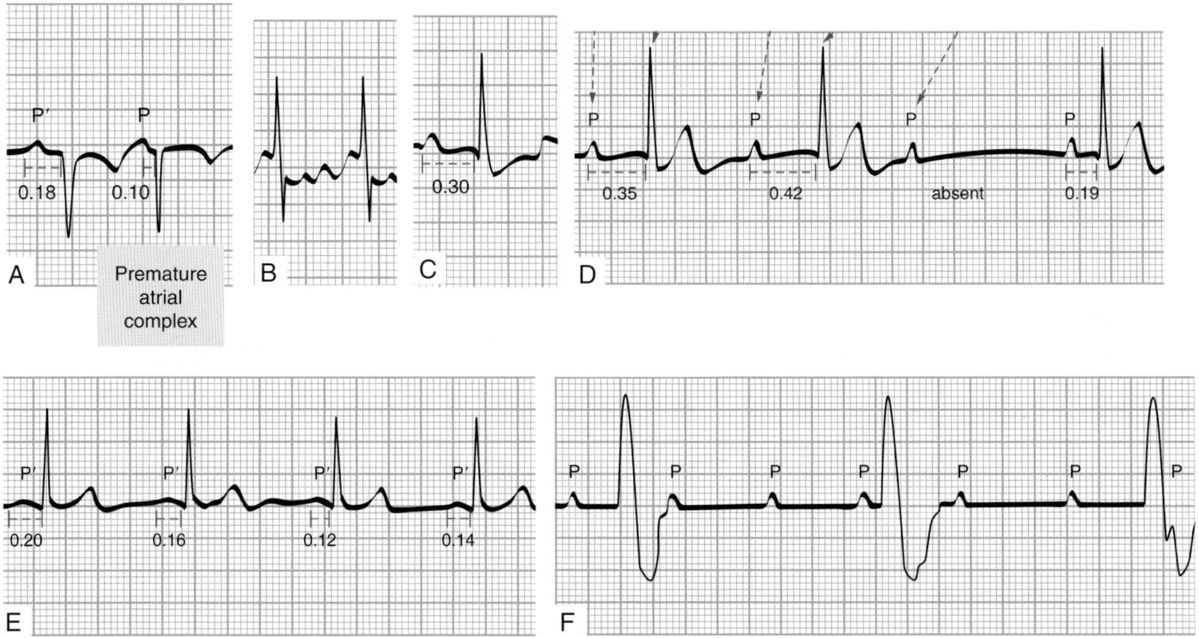

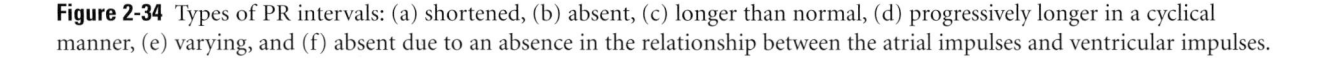

Figure 2-34 Types of PR intervals: (a) shortened, (b) absent, (c) longer than normal, (d) progressively longer in a cyclical manner, (e) varying, and (f) absent due to an absence in the relationship between the atrial impulses and ventricular impulses.

Sinus Dysrhythmias

3

What is in this chapter

- Normal sinus rhythm characteristics
- Sinus bradycardia characteristics
- Sinus tachycardia characteristics
- Sinus dysrhythmia characteristics
- Sinus arrest characteristics

Characteristics common to sinus dysrhythmias

- Arise from SA node.
- Normal P wave precedes each QRS complex.
- PR intervals are normal at 0.12 to 0.20 seconds in duration.
- QRS complexes are normal.

Normal sinus rhythm characteristics

Rate:	60 to 100 beats per minute
Regularity:	It is regular
P waves:	Present and normal; all the P waves are followed by a QRS complex
QRS complexes:	Normal
PR interval:	Within normal range (0.12 to 0.20 seconds)
QT interval:	Within normal range (0.36 to 0.44 seconds)

Figure 3-1

Summary of characteristics of normal sinus rhythm.

Normal sinus rhythm arises from the SA node. Each impulse travels down through the conduction system in a normal manner.

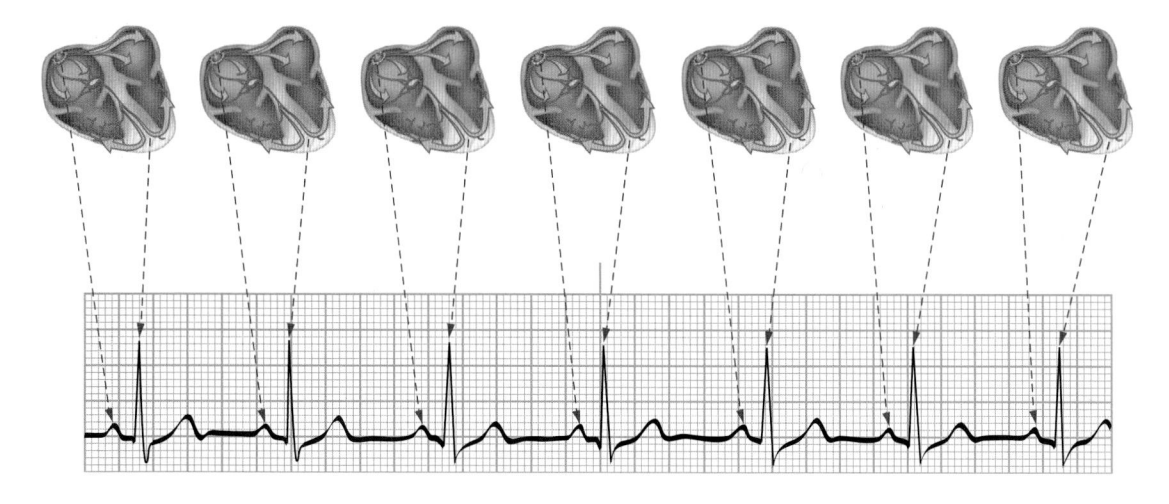

Figure 3-2
Normal sinus rhythm.

Sinus bradycardia characteristics

Rate:	Less than 60 beats per minute
Regularity:	It is regular
P waves:	Present and normal; all the P waves are followed by a QRS complex
QRS complexes:	Normal
PR interval:	Within normal range (0.12 to 0.20 seconds)
QT interval:	Within normal range (0.36 to 0.44 seconds) but may be prolonged

Figure 3-3
Summary of characteristics of sinus bradycardia.

Sinus bradycardia arises from the SA node. Each impulse travels down through the conduction system in a normal manner.

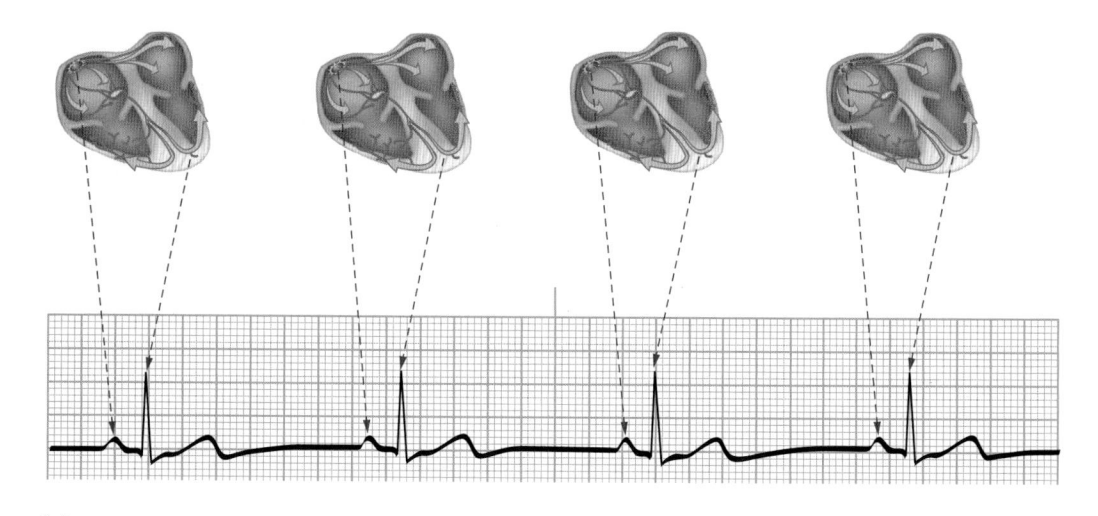

Figure 3-4
Sinus bradycardia.

Sinus tachycardia characteristics

Rate:	100 to 160 beats per minute
Regularity:	It is regular
P waves:	Present and normal; all the P waves are followed by a QRS complex
QRS complexes:	Normal
PR interval:	Within normal range (0.12 to 0.20 seconds)
QT interval:	Within normal range (0.36 to 0.44 seconds) but commonly shortened

Figure 3-5
Summary of characteristics of sinus tachycardia.

Sinus tachycardia arises from the SA node. Each impulse travels down through the conduction system in a normal manner.

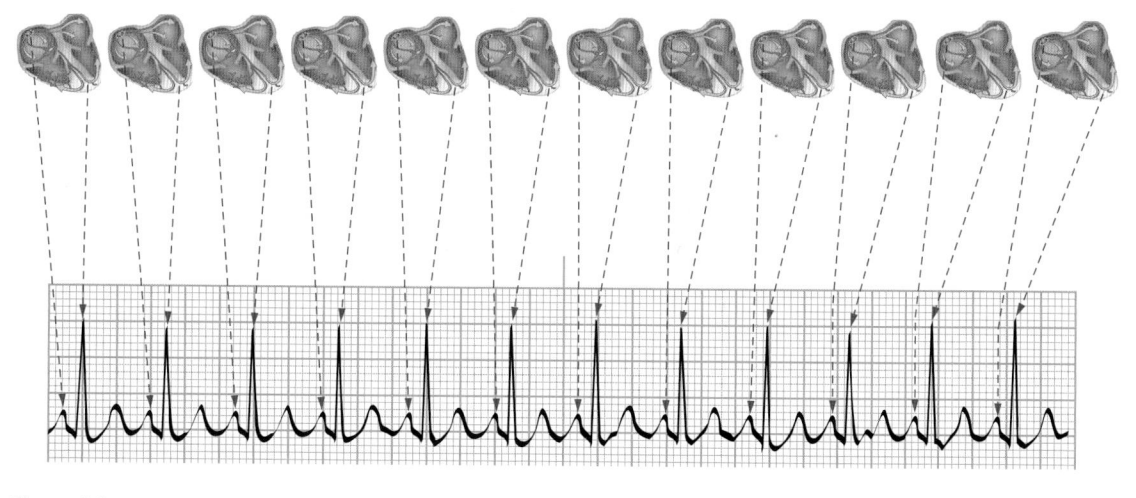

Figure 3-6
Sinus tachycardia.

Sinus dysrhythmia characteristics

Rate:	Typically 60 to 100 beats per minute
Regularity:	It is regularly irregular (patterned irregularity); seems to speed up, slow down, and speed up in a cyclical fashion
P waves:	Present and normal; all the P waves are followed by a QRS complex
QRS complexes:	Normal
PR interval:	Within normal range (0.12 to 0.20 seconds)
QT interval:	May vary slightly but usually within normal range (0.36 to 0.44 seconds)

Figure 3-7
Summary of characteristics of sinus dysrhythmia.

Sinus dysrhythmia arises from the SA node. Each impulse travels down through the conduction system in a normal manner.

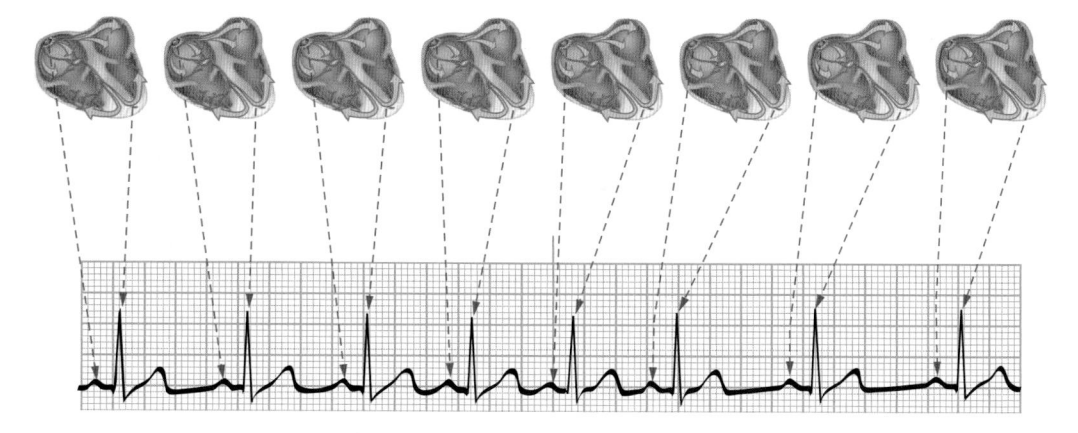

Figure 3-8
Sinus dysrhythmia.

Sinus arrest characteristics

Rate:	Typically 60 to 100 beats per minute, but may be slower depending on frequency and length of arrest
Regularity:	It is irregular where there is a pause in the rhythm (the SA node fails to initiate a beat)
P waves:	Present and normal; all the P waves are followed by a QRS complex
QRS complexes:	Normal
PR interval:	Within normal range (0.12 to 0.20 seconds)
QT interval:	Within normal range (0.36 to 0.44 seconds); unmeasurable during a pause

Figure 3-9
Summary of characteristics of sinus arrest.

Sinus arrest occurs when the SA node fails to initiate an impulse.

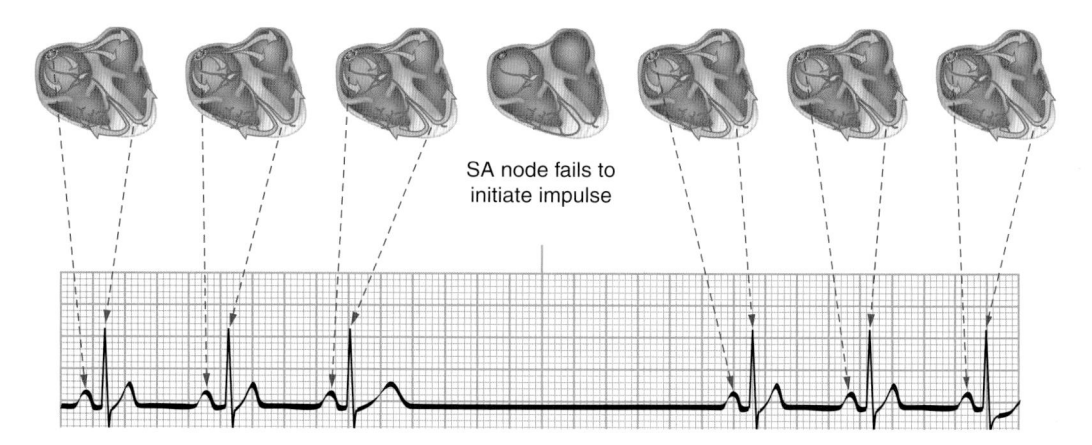

SA node fails to
initiate impulse

Figure 3-10
Summary of characteristics of sinus arrest.

Atrial Dysrhythmias

4

What is in this chapter

- Premature atrial complexes (PACs) characteristics
- Wandering atrial pacemaker characteristics
- Atrial tachycardia characteristics
- Multifocal atrial tachycardia characteristics
- Atrial flutter characteristics
- Atrial fibrillatrion characteristics

Characteristics common to atrial dysrhythmias

- Arise from atrial tissue or internodal pathways.
- P' waves (if present) that differ in appearance from normal sinus P waves precede each QRS complex.
- P'R intervals may be normal, shortened, or prolonged.
- QRS complexes are normal (unless there is also an interventricular conduction defect or aberrancy).

Wandering atrial pacemaker characteristics

Rate:	Usually within normal limits
Regularity:	Slightly irregular
P waves:	Continuously change in appearance
QRS complexes:	Normal
PR interval:	Varies
QT interval:	Usually within normal limits but may vary

Figure 4-1
Summary of characteristics of wandering atrial pacemaker.

Wandering atrial pacemaker arises from different sites in the atria.

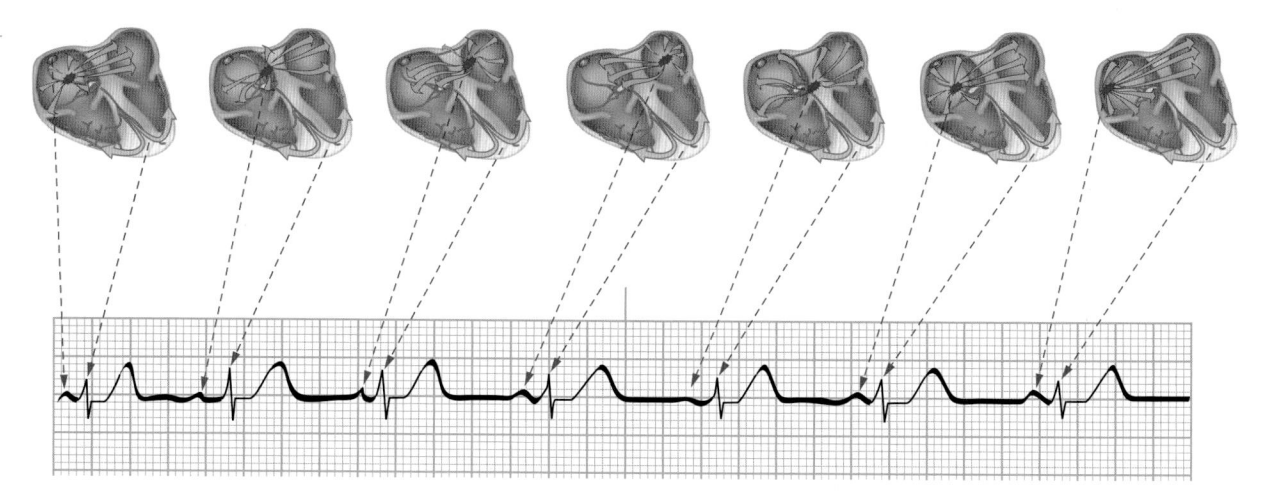

Figure 4-2
Wandering atrial pacemaker.

Premature atrial complexes (PAC) characteristics

Rate:	Depends on the underlying rhythm
Regularity:	May be occasionally irregular or frequently irregular (depends on the number of PACs present). It may also be seen as patterned irregularity if bigeminal, trigeminal, or quadrigeminal PACs are seen.
P waves:	May be upright or inverted, will appear different than those of the underlying rhythm
QRS complexes:	Normal
PR interval:	Will be normal duration if ectopic beat arises from the upper- or middle-right atrium. It is shorter than 0.12 seconds in duration if the ectopic impulse arises from the lower right atrium or in the upper part of the AV junction. In some cases it can also be prolonged
QT interval:	Usually within normal limits but may vary

Figure 4-3

Summary of characteristics of premature atrial complexes.

Premature atrial complexes arise from somewhere in the atrium.

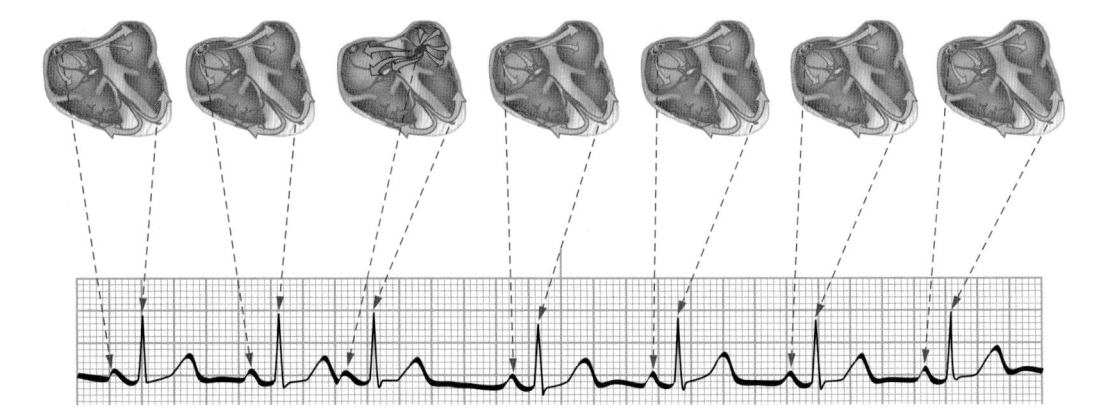

Figure 4-4
Premature atrial complexes.

The pause that follows a premature beat is called a noncompensatory pause if the space between the complex before and after the premature beat is less than the sum of two R-R intervals.

Non-compensatory pauses are typically seen with premature atrial and junctional complexes (PACs, PJCs).

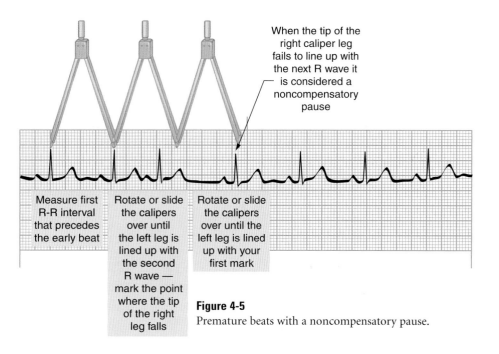

When the tip of the right caliper leg fails to line up with the next R wave it is considered a noncompensatory pause

Measure first R-R interval that precedes the early beat

Rotate or slide the calipers over until the left leg is lined up with the second R wave — mark the point where the tip of the right leg falls

Rotate or slide the calipers over until the left leg is lined up with your first mark

Figure 4-5
Premature beats with a noncompensatory pause.

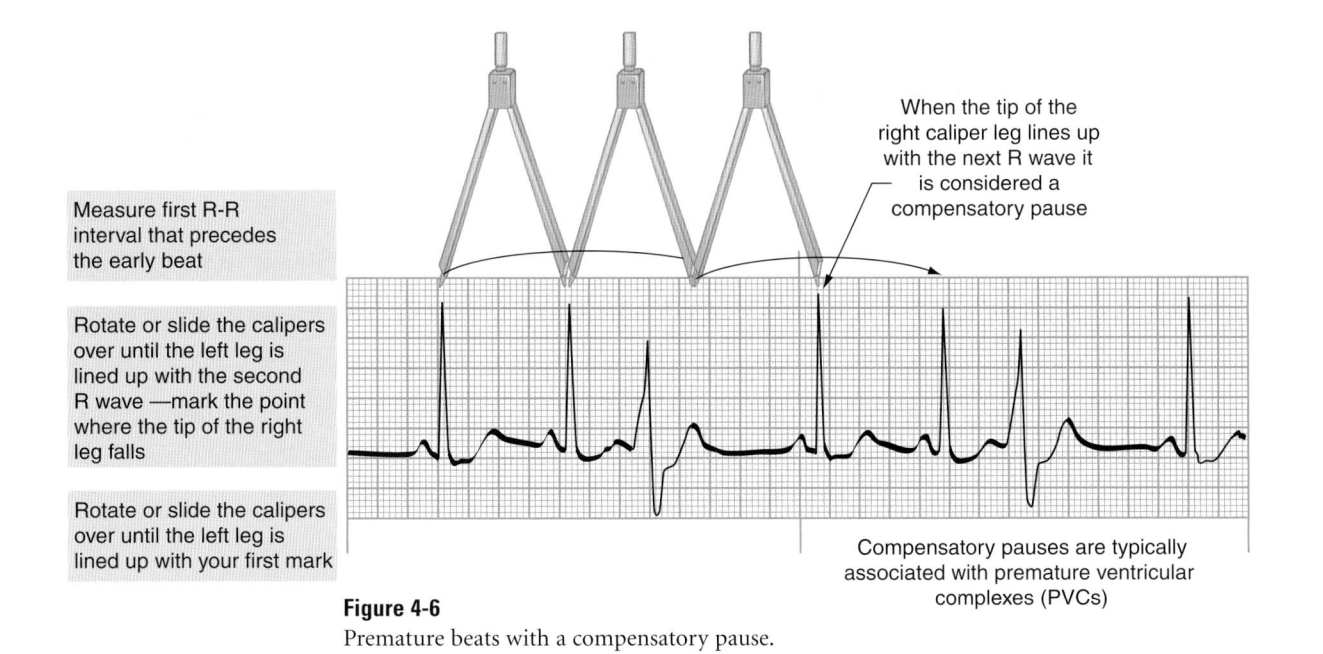

When the tip of the right caliper leg lines up with the next R wave it is considered a compensatory pause

Measure first R-R interval that precedes the early beat

Rotate or slide the calipers over until the left leg is lined up with the second R wave —mark the point where the tip of the right leg falls

Rotate or slide the calipers over until the left leg is lined up with your first mark

Compensatory pauses are typically associated with premature ventricular complexes (PVCs)

Figure 4-6
Premature beats with a compensatory pause.

Premature beats occurring in a pattern

One way to describe PACs is how they are intermingled among the normal beats. When every other beat is a PAC, it is called bigeminal PACs, or atrial bigeminy. If every third beat is a PAC, it is called trigeminal PACs, or atrial trigeminy. Likewise, if a PAC occurs every fourth beat, it is called quadrigeminal PACs, or atrial quadrigeminy. Regular PACs at greater intervals than every fourth beat have no special name.

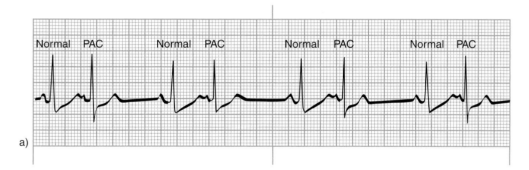

Figure 4-7
Premature atrial complexes: (a) bigeminal PACs, (b) trigeminal PACs, and (c) quadrigeminal PACs.

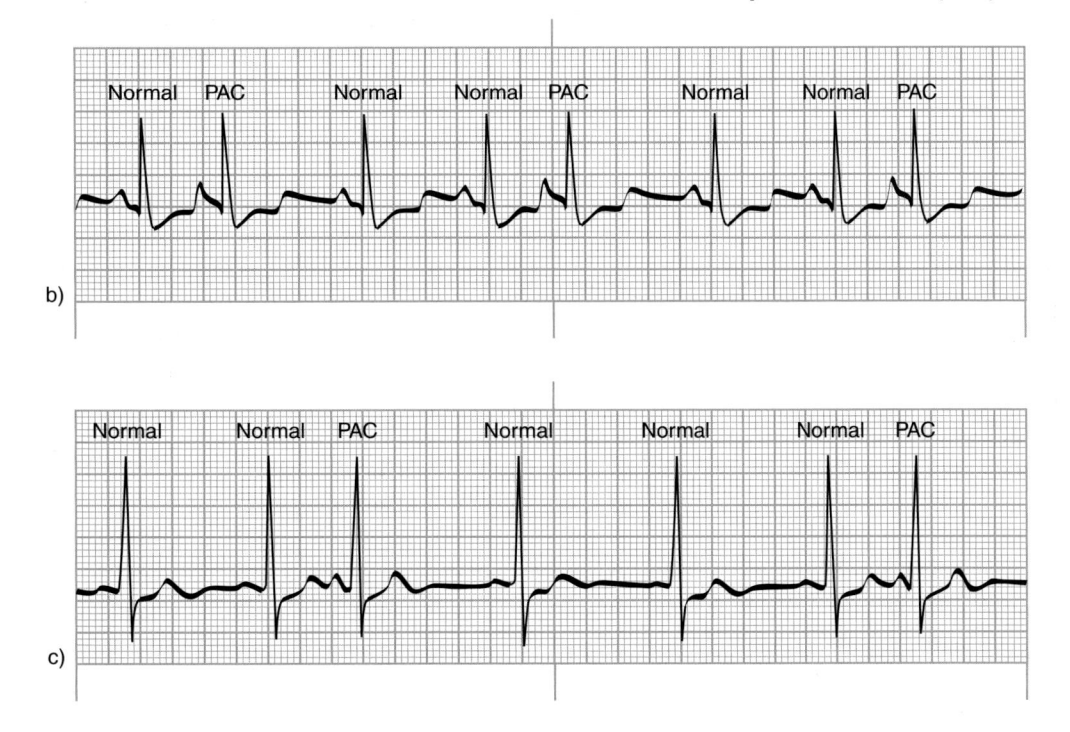

b)

c)

Atrial tachycardia characteristics

Rate:	150 to 250 beats per minute
Regularity:	Regular unless the onset is witnessed (thereby producing paroxysmal irregularity)
P waves:	May be upright or inverted, will appear different than those of the underlying rhythm
QRS complexes:	Normal
PR interval:	Will be normal duration if ectopic beat arises from the upper- or middle-right atrium. It is shorter than 0.12 seconds in duration if the ectopic impulse arises from the lower-right atrium or in the upper part of the AV junction
QT interval:	Usually within normal limits but may be shorter due to the rapid rate

Narrow complex tachycardia that has a sudden, witnessed onset and abrupt termination is called paroxysmal tachycardia.

Narrow complex tachycardia that cannot be clearly identified as atrial or junctional tachycardia is referred to as supraventricular tachycardia.

Figure 4-8
Summary of characteristics of atrial tachycardia.

Atrial tachycardia arises from a single focus in the atria.

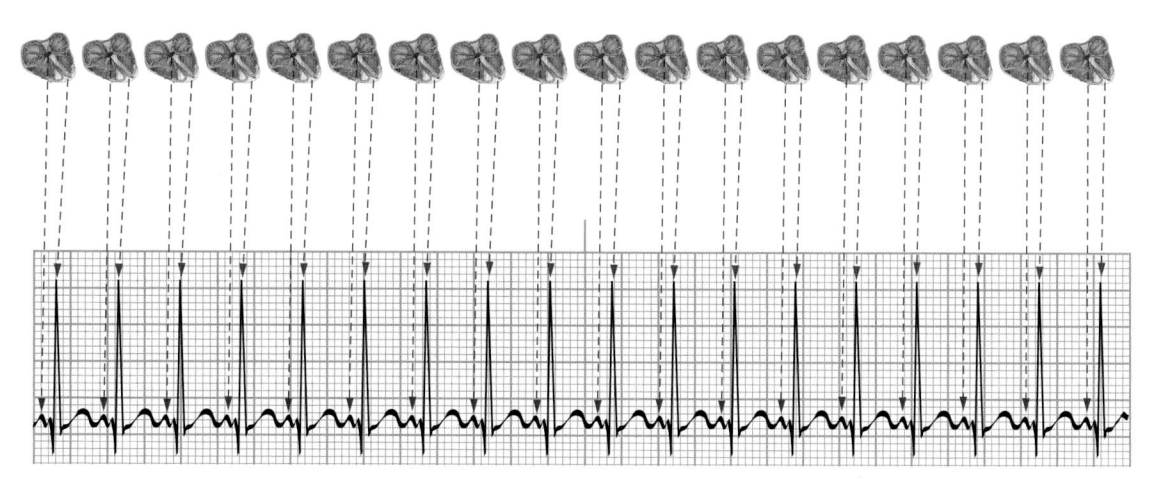

Figure 4-9
Atrial tachycardia.

Multifocal atrial tachycardia characteristics

Rate:	120 to 150 beats per minute
Regularity:	Irregular
P waves:	P′ waves change in morphology (appearance) from beat to beat (at least three different shapes)
QRS complexes:	Normal
PR interval:	Varies
QT interval:	Usually within normal limits but may vary

Figure 4-10
Summary of characteristics of multifocal atrial tachycardia.

In multifocal atrial tachycardia, the pacemaker site shifts between the SA node, atria, and/or the AV junction.

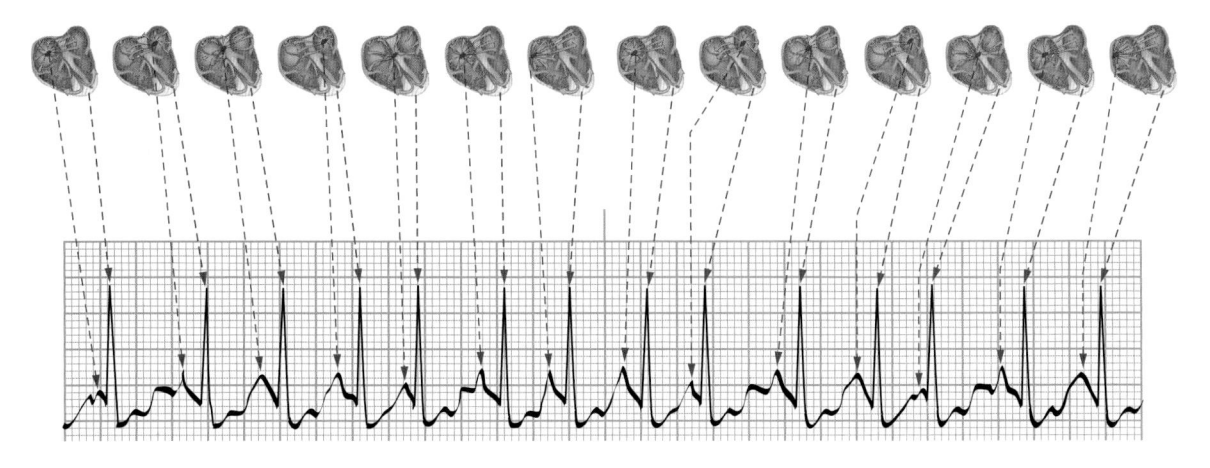

Figure 4-11
Multifocal atrial tachycardia.

Atrial flutter characteristics

Rate:	Ventricular rate may be slow, normal, or fast; atrial rate is between 250 and 350 beats per minute
Regularity:	May be regular or irregular (depending on whether the conduction ratio stays the same or varies)
P waves:	Absent, instead there are flutter waves; the ratio of atrial waveforms to QRS complexes may be 2:1, 3:1, or 4:1. An atrial-to-ventricular conduction ratio of 1:1 is rare
QRS complexes:	Normal
PR interval:	Not measurable
QT interval:	Not measurable

Figure 4-12
Summary of characteristics of atrial flutter.

Atrial flutter arises from rapid depolarization of a single focus in the atria.

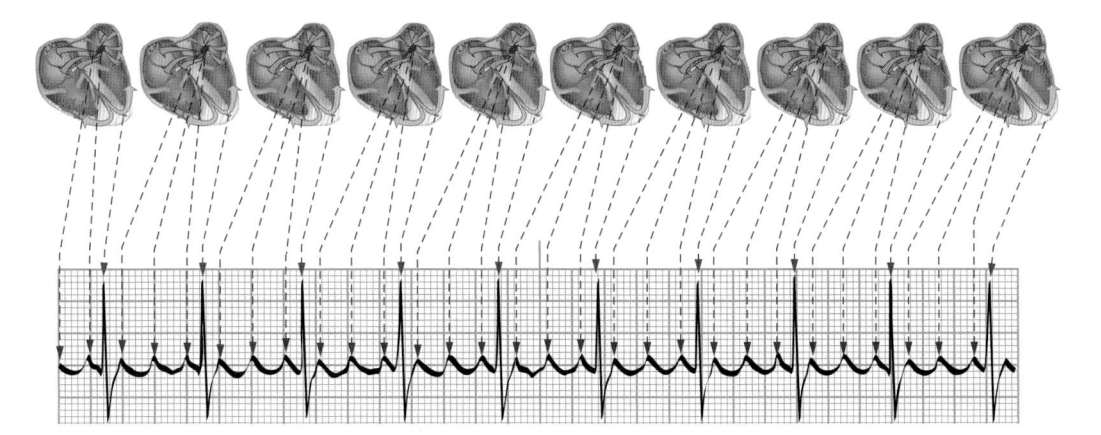

Figure 4-13
Atrial flutter.

Atrial fibrillation characteristics

Rate:	Ventricular rate may be slow, normal, or fast; atrial rate is greater than 350 beats per minute
Regularity:	Totally (chaotically) irregular
P waves:	Absent; instead there is a chaotic-looking baseline
QRS complexes:	Normal
PR interval:	Absent
QT interval:	Unmeasurable

Figure 4-14
Summary of characteristics of atrial fibrillation.

Atrial fibrillation arises from many different sites in the atria.

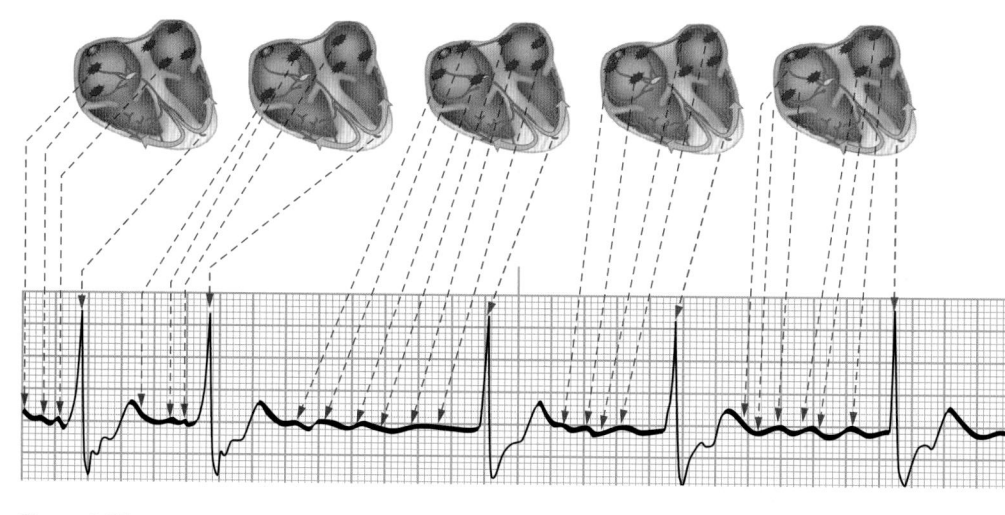

Figure 4-15
Atrial fibrillation.

Junctional Dysrhythmias

5

What is in this chapter

- Premature junctional complexes (PJCs) characteristics
- Junctional escape rhythm characteristics
- Accelerated junctional rhythm characteristics
- Junctional tachycardia characteristics

Characteristics common to junctional dysrhythmias

- Arise from the AV junction, the area around the AV node, or the bundle of His.
- P' wave may be inverted (when they would otherwise be upright) with a short P'R interval (less than 0.12 seconds in duration).
- Alternatively, the P' wave may be absent (as it is buried by the QRS complex), or it may follow the QRS complex. If the P' wave is buried in the QRS complex it can change the morphology of the QRS complex.
- If present, P'R intervals are shortened.
- QRS complexes are normal (unless there is an interventricular conduction defect or aberrancy).

Premature junctional complexes (PJCs) characteristics

Rate:	Depends on the underlying rhythm
Regularity:	May be occasionally irregular or frequently irregular (depends on the number of PJCs present). It may also be seen as patterned irregularity if bigeminal, trigeminal, or quadrigeminal PJCs are seen.
P waves:	Inverted—may immediately precede, occur during (absent), or follow the QRS complex
QRS complexes:	Normal
PR interval:	Will be shorter than normal if the P′ wave precedes the QRS complex and absent if the P′ wave is buried in the QRS; referred to as the RP′ interval if the P′ wave follows the QRS complex
QT interval:	Usually within normal limits

Figure 5-1
Summary of characteristics of premature junctional complexes (PJCs).

PJCs are typically followed by a non-compensatory pause.

Premature junctional complex arises from somewhere in the AV junction.

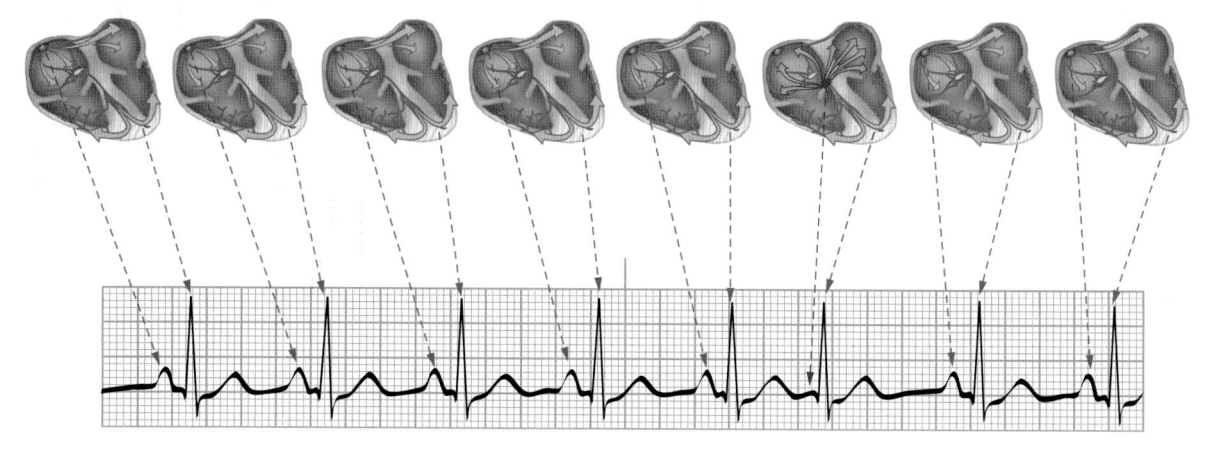

Figure 5-2
Summary of characteristics of premature junctional complexes (PJCs).

Junctional escape rhythm characteristics

Rate:	40 to 60 beats per minute
Regularity:	Regular
P waves:	Inverted—may immediately precede, occur during (absent), or follow the QRS complex
QRS complexes:	Normal
PR interval:	Will be shorter than normal if the P'wave precedes the QRS complex and absent if the P' wave is buried in the QRS; referred to as the RP' interval if the P' wave follows the QRS complex
QT interval:	Usually within normal limits

Figure 5-3

Summary of characteristics of junctional escape rhythm.

Junctional escape rhythm arises from a single site in the AV junction.

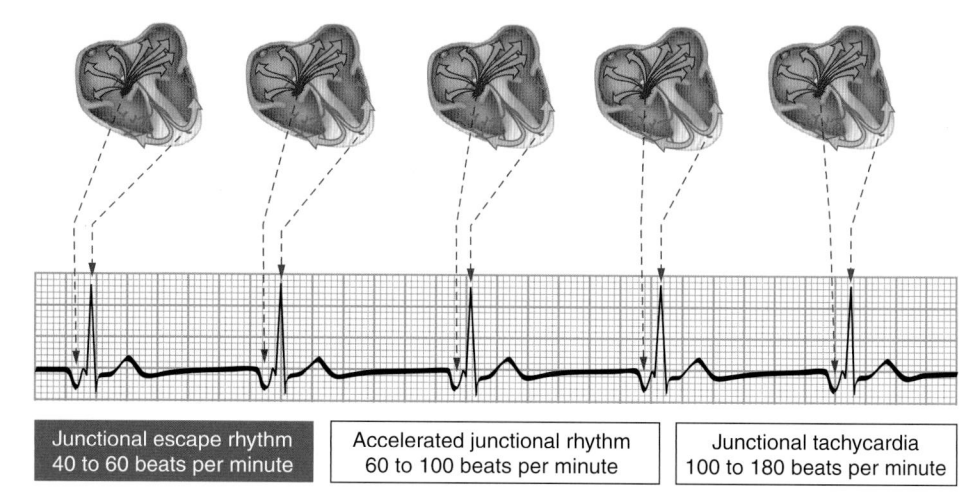

| Junctional escape rhythm 40 to 60 beats per minute | Accelerated junctional rhythm 60 to 100 beats per minute | Junctional tachycardia 100 to 180 beats per minute |

Figure 5-4
Junctional escape rhythm.

Accelerated junctional rhythm characteristics

Rate:	60 to 100 beats per minute
Regularity:	Regular
P waves:	Inverted—may immediately precede, occur during (absent), or follow the QRS complex
QRS complexes:	Normal
PR interval:	Will be shorter than normal if the P′ wave precedes the QRS complex and absent if the P′ wave is buried in the QRS; referred to as the RP′ interval if the P′ wave follows the QRS complex
QT interval:	Usually within normal limits

Figure 5-5

Summary of characteristics of accelerated junctional rhythm.

Accelerated junctional rhythm arises from a single site in the AV junction.

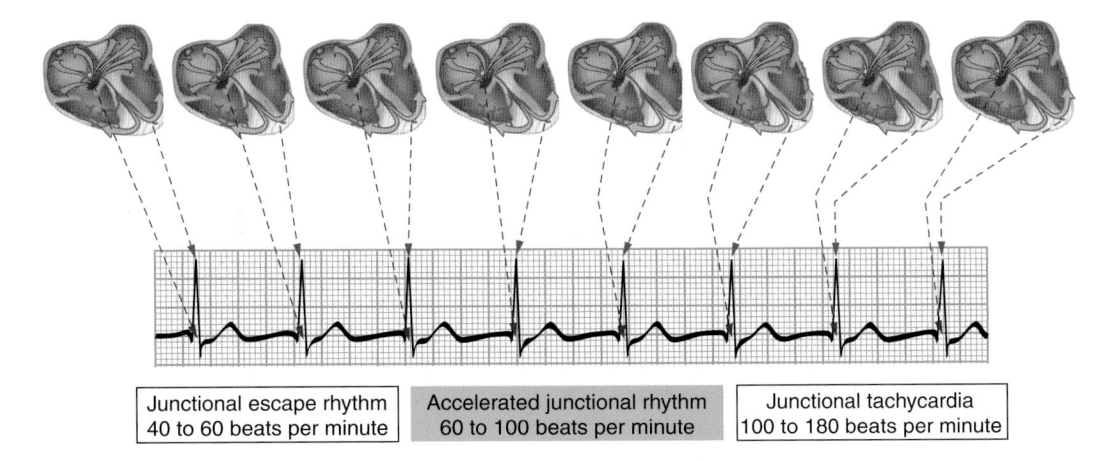

| Junctional escape rhythm | Accelerated junctional rhythm | Junctional tachycardia |
| 40 to 60 beats per minute | 60 to 100 beats per minute | 100 to 180 beats per minute |

Figure 5-6
Accelerated junctional rhythm.

Junctional tachycardia characteristics

Rate:	100 to 180 beats per minute
Regularity:	Regular
P waves:	Inverted—may immediately precede, occur during (absent), or follow the QRS complex
QRS complexes:	Normal
PR interval:	Will be shorter than normal if the P′ wave precedes the QRS complex and absent if the P′ wave is buried in the QRS; referred to as the RP′ interval if the P′ wave follows the QRS complex
QT interval:	Usually within normal limits

Figure 5-7
Summary of characteristics of junctional tachycardia.

Junctional tachycardia arises from a single focus in the AV junction.

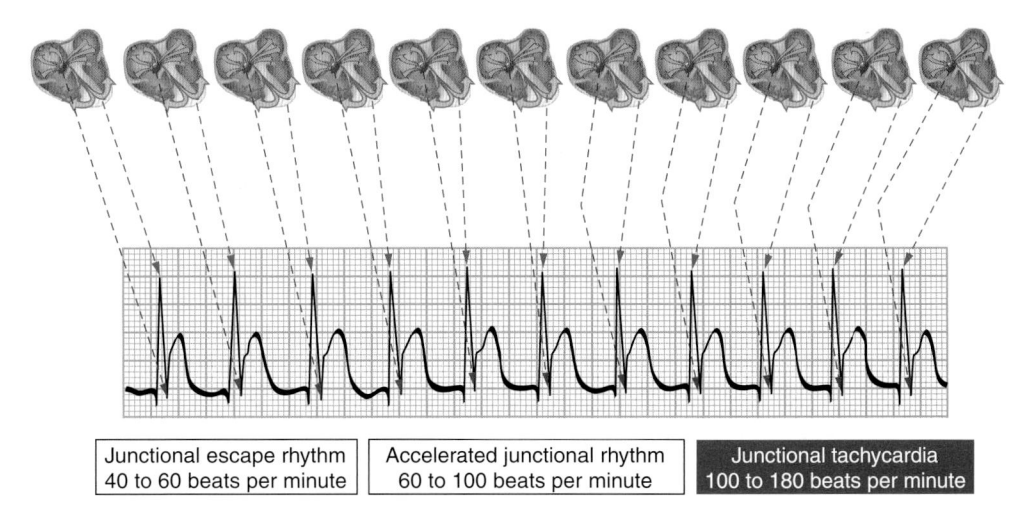

| Junctional escape rhythm 40 to 60 beats per minute | Accelerated junctional rhythm 60 to 100 beats per minute | Junctional tachycardia 100 to 180 beats per minute |

Figure 5-8
Junctional tachycardia.

Ventricular Dysrhythmias

6

What is in this chapter

- Premature ventricular complexes (PVCs) characteristics
- Idioventricular rhythm characteristics
- Accelerated idioventricular rhythm characteristics
- Ventricular tachycardia characteristics

Characteristics common to ventricular dysrhythmias

- Arise from the ventricles below the bundle of His.
- QRS complexes are wide (greater than 0.12 seconds in duration) and bizarre looking.
- Ventricular beats have T waves in the opposite direction of the R wave.
- P waves are not visible as they are hidden in the QRS complexes.

Premature ventricular complexes (PVCs) characteristics

Rate:	Depends on the underlying rhythm
Regularity:	May be occasionally irregular or frequently irregular (depends on the number of PVCs present). It may also be seen as patterned irregularity if bigeminal, trigeminal, or quadrigeminal PVCs are seen.
P waves:	Not preceded by a P wave (if seen, they are dissociated)
QRS complexes:	Wide, large, and bizarre looking
PR interval:	Not measurable
QT interval:	Usually prolonged with the PVC

Figure 6-1

Summary of characteristics of premature ventricular complexes.

PVCs are followed by a compensatory pause.

Sometimes, PVCs originate from only one location in the ventricle. These beats look the same and are called uniform (also referred to as unifocal) PVCs. Other times, PVCs arise from different sites in the ventricles. These beats tend to look different from each other and are called multiformed (multifocal) PVCs.

Premature ventricular complexes arise from somewhere in the ventricle(s).

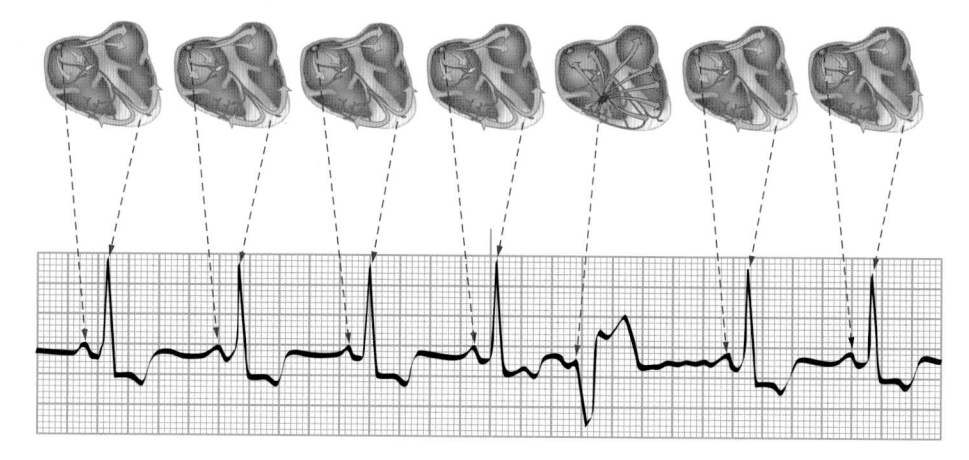

Figure 6-2
Premature ventricular complexes (PVCs).

PVCs that occur one after the other (two PVCs in a row) are called a couplet, or pair.

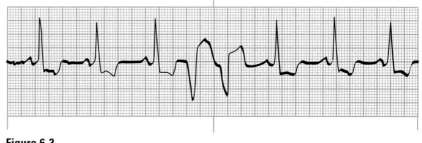

Figure 6-3
Couplet of PVCs.

Three or more PVCs in a row at a ventricular rate of at least 100 BPM is called ventricular tachycardia. It may be called a salvo, run, or burst of ventricular tachycardia.

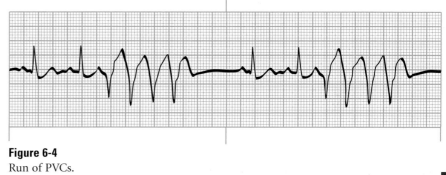

Figure 6-4
Run of PVCs.

An interpolated PVC occurs when a PVC does not disrupt the normal cardiac cycle. It appears as a PVC squeezed between two regular complexes.

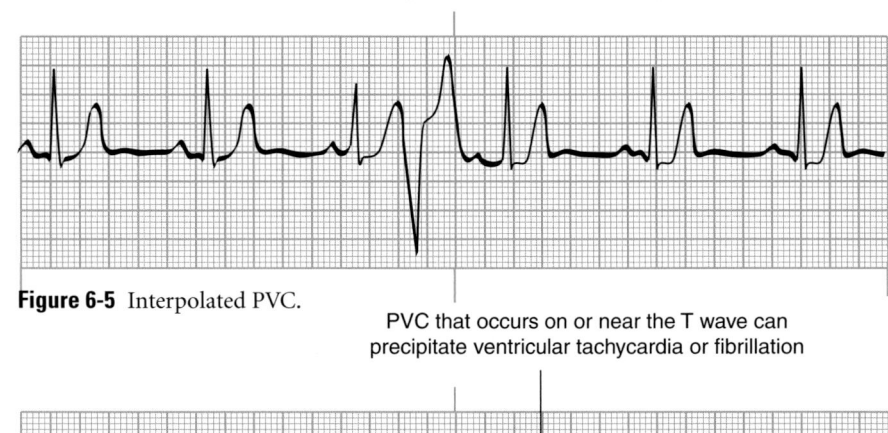

Figure 6-5 Interpolated PVC.

PVC that occurs on or near the T wave can precipitate ventricular tachycardia or fibrillation

A PVC occurring on or near the previous T wave is called an R-on-T PVC.

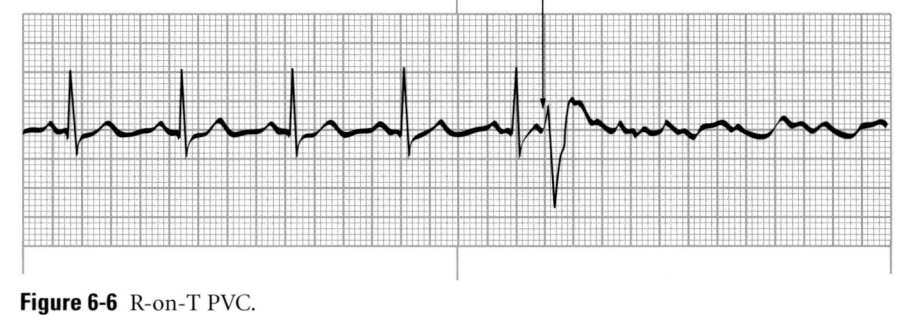

Figure 6-6 R-on-T PVC.

Idioventricular rhythm characteristics

Rate:	20 to 40 beats per minute (may be slower)
Regularity:	Regular
P waves:	Not preceded by a P wave (if seen, they are dissociated and would therefore be a 3rd-degree heart block with an idioventricular escape)
QRS complexes:	Wide, large, and bizarre looking
PR interval:	Not measurable
QT interval:	Usually prolonged

Figure 6-7
Summary of characteristics of idioventricular rhythm.

Idioventricular rhythm arises from a single site in the ventricles(s).

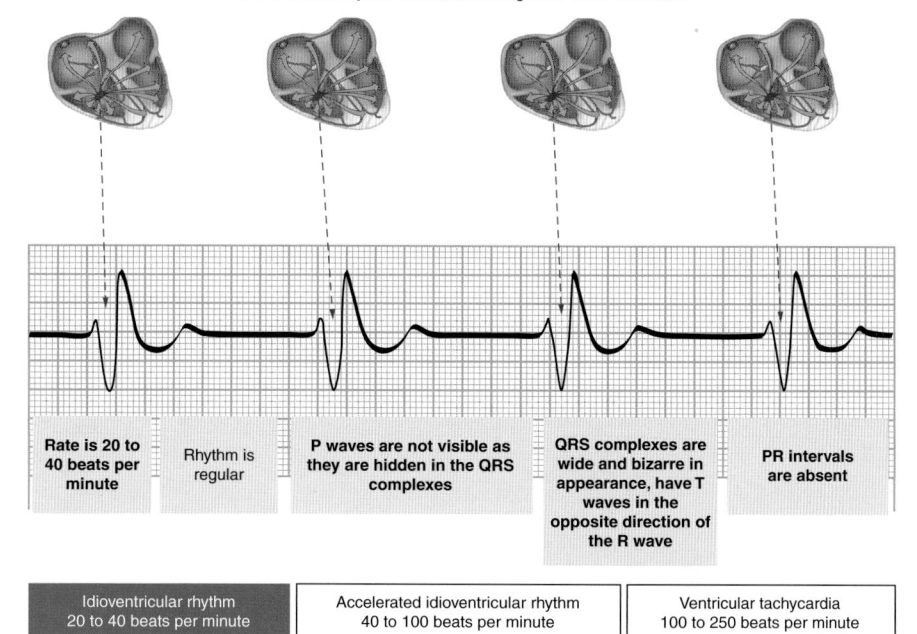

Idioventricular rhythm arises from a single site in the ventricles.

Rate is 20 to 40 beats per minute

Rhythm is regular

P waves are not visible as they are hidden in the QRS complexes

QRS complexes are wide and bizarre in appearance, have T waves in the opposite direction of the R wave

PR intervals are absent

Idioventricular rhythm 20 to 40 beats per minute

Accelerated idioventricular rhythm 40 to 100 beats per minute

Ventricular tachycardia 100 to 250 beats per minute

Figure 6-8
Idioventricular rhythm.

Accelerated idioventricular rhythm characteristics

Rate:	40 to 100 beats per minute
Regularity:	Regular
P waves:	Not preceded by a P wave
QRS complexes:	Wide, large, and bizarre looking
PR interval:	Not measurable
QT interval:	Usually prolonged

Figure 6-9

Summary of characteristics of accelerated idioventricular rhythm.

Accelerated idioventricular rhythm arises from a single site in the ventricles(s).

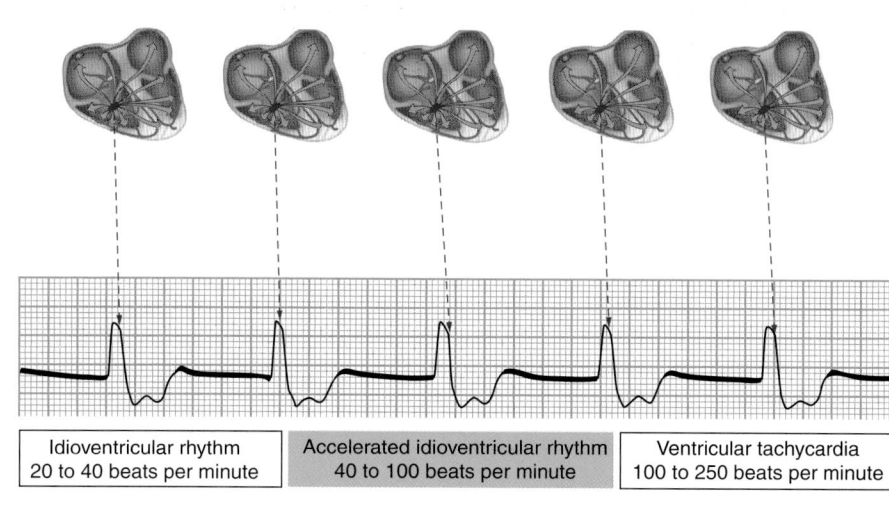

| Idioventricular rhythm 20 to 40 beats per minute | Accelerated idioventricular rhythm 40 to 100 beats per minute | Ventricular tachycardia 100 to 250 beats per minute |

Figure 6-10
Accelerated idioventricular rhythm.

Ventricular tachycardia characteristics

Rate:	100 to 250 beats per minute
Regularity:	Regular
P waves:	Not preceded by a P wave (if seen, they are dissociated)
QRS complexes:	Wide, large, and bizarre looking
PR interval:	Not measurable
QT interval:	Not measurable

Figure 6-11
Summary of characteristics of ventricular tachycardia.

Ventricular tachycardia may be monomorphic, where the appearance of each QRS complex is similar, or polymorphic, where the appearance varies considerably from complex to complex.

Ventricular tachycardia arises from a single site in the ventricles(s).

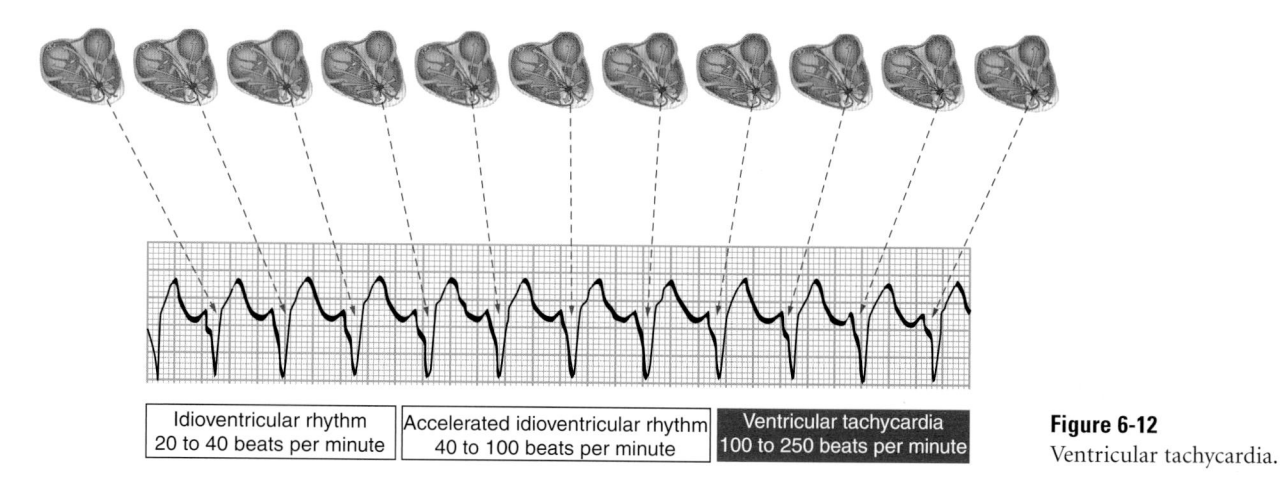

Idioventricular rhythm 20 to 40 beats per minute	Accelerated idioventricular rhythm 40 to 100 beats per minute	Ventricular tachycardia 100 to 250 beats per minute

Figure 6-12
Ventricular tachycardia.

Two other conditions to be familiar with:

Ventricular fibrillation (VF)—results from chaotic firing of multiple sites in the ventricles. This causes the heart muscle to quiver, much like a handful of worms, rather than contracting efficiently. On the ECG monitor it appears like a wavy line, totally chaotic, without any logic.

Asystole—is the absense of any cardiac activity. It appears as a flat (or nearly flat) line on the monitor screen.

AV Heart Blocks

7

What is in this chapter

- 1st-degree AV heart block characteristics
- 2nd-degree AV heart block, Type I (Wenckebach) characteristics
- 2nd-degree AV heart block, Type II characteristics
- 3rd-degree AV heart block characteristics

Characteristics common to AV heart blocks

- P waves are upright and round. In 1st-degree AV block all the P waves are followed by a QRS complex. In 2nd-degree AV block not all the P waves are followed by a QRS complex, and in 3rd-degree block there is no relationship between the P waves and QRS complexes.
- In 1st-degree AV block PR interval is longer than normal and constant. In 2nd-degree AV block, Type I, in a cyclical manner the PR interval is progressively longer until a QRS complex is dropped. In 2nd-degree AV block, Type II, the PR interval of the conducted beats is constant. In 3rd-degree block there is no PR interval.
- QRS complexes may be normal or wide.

1st-degree AV heart block characteristics

Rate:	Underlying rate may be slow, normal, or fast
Regularity:	Underlying rhythm is usually regular
P waves:	Present and normal and all are followed by a QRS complex
QRS complexes:	Should be normal
PR interval:	Longer than 0.20 seconds and is constant (the same each time)
QT interval:	Usually within normal limits

Figure 7-1
Summary of characteristics of 1st-degree AV block.

In 1st-degree AV heart block impulses arise from the SA node but their passage through the AV node is delayed.

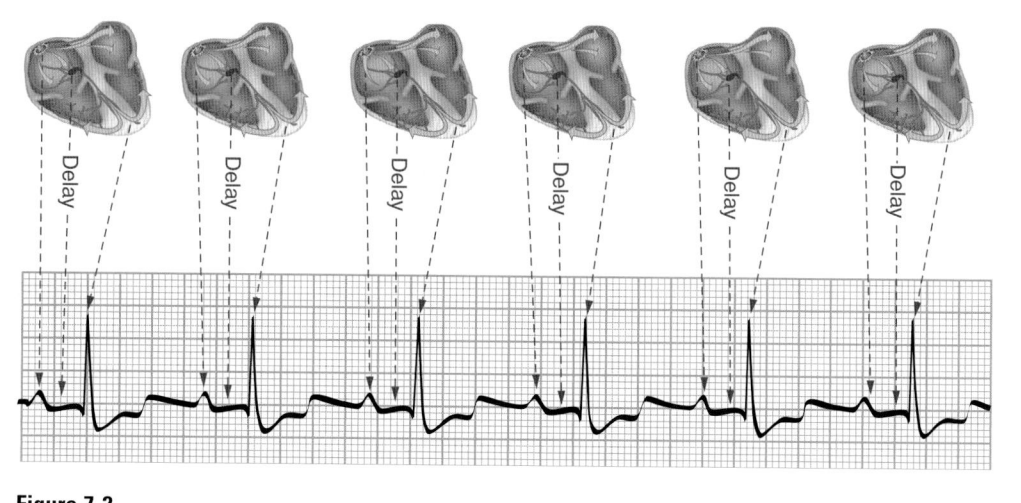

Figure 7-2
1st-degree AV block.

2nd-degree AV heart block, Type I (Wenckebach) characteristics

Rate:	Ventricular rate may be slow, normal, or fast; atrial rate is within normal range
Regularity:	Patterned irregularity
P waves:	Present and normal; not all the P waves are followed by a QRS complex
QRS complexes:	Should be normal
PR interval:	Progressively longer until a QRS complex is dropped; the cycle then begins again
QT interval:	Usually within normal limits

Figure 7-3
Summary of characteristics of 2nd-degree AV block, Type I.

In 2nd-degree AV heart block, Type I (Wenckebach), impulses arise from the SA node but their passage through the AV node is progressively delayed until the impulse is blocked.

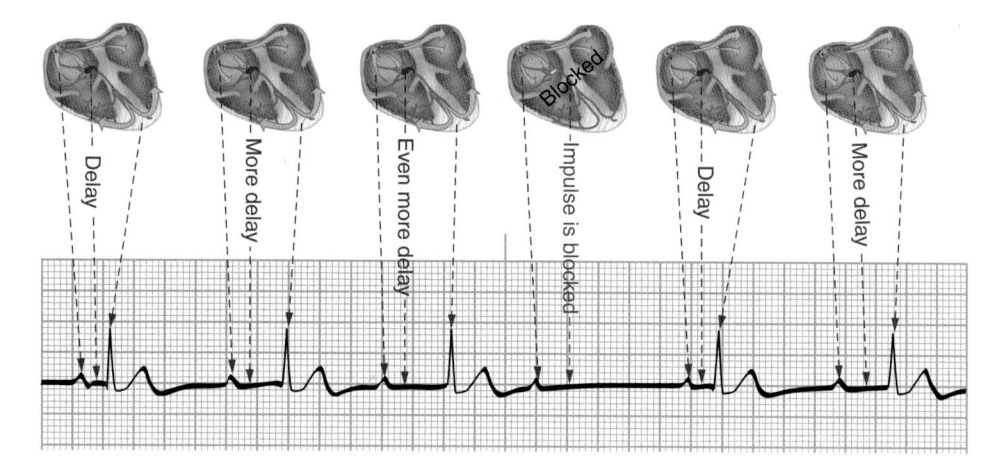

Figure 7-4
2nd-degree AV block, Type I.

2nd-degree AV heart block, Type II characteristics

Rate:	Ventricular rate may be slow, normal, or fast; atrial rate is within normal range
Regularity:	May be regular or irregular (depends on whether conduction ratio remains the same)
P waves:	Present and normal; not all the P waves are followed by a QRS complex
QRS complexes:	Should be normal
PR interval:	Constant for all conducted beats
QT interval:	Usually within normal limits

Figure 7-5

Summary of characteristics of 2nd-degree AV block, Type II.

In 2nd-degree AV heart block, Type II, impulses arise from the SA node but some are blocked in the bundle of His or bundle branches.

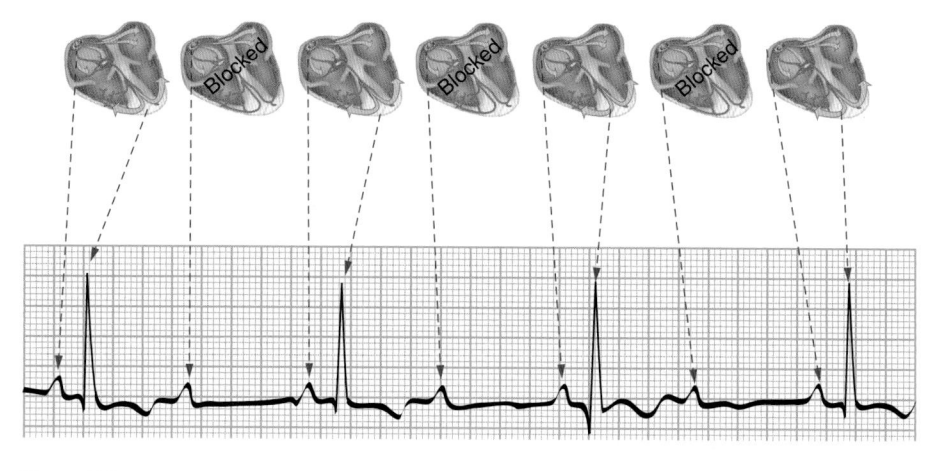

Figure 7-6
2nd-degree AV block, Type II.

3rd-degree AV heart block characteristics

Rate:	Ventricular rate may be slow, normal, or fast; atrial rate is within normal range
Regularity:	Atrial rhythm and ventricular rhythms are regular but not related to one another
P waves:	Present and normal; not related to the QRS complexes; appear to march through the QRS complexes
QRS complexes:	Normal if escape focus is junctional and widened if escape focus is ventricular
PR interval:	Not measurable
QT interval:	May or may not be within normal limits

Figure 7-7
Summary of characteristics of 3rd-degree AV block.

In 3rd-degree AV heart block there is a complete block at the AV node resulting in the atria being depolarized by an impulse that arises from the SA node and the ventricles being depolarized by an escape pacemaker that arises somewhere below the AV node.

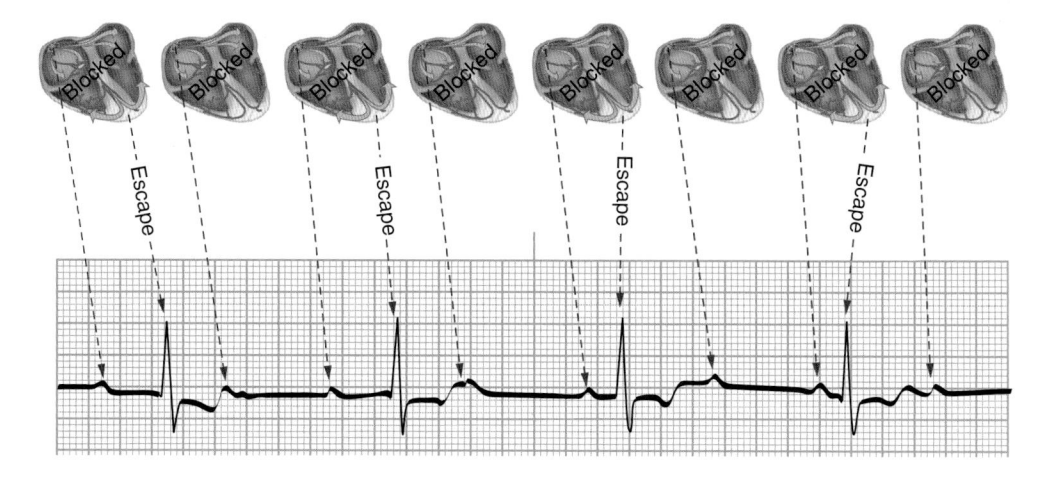

Figure 7-8
3rd-degree AV block.

Electrical Axis

8

What is in this chapter

- Direction of ECG waveforms
- Mean QRS Vector
- Methods for Determining QRS axis

- Lead I
- Lead aV$_F$
- Axis Deviation

Direction of ECG waveforms

- Depolarization and repolarization of the cardiac cells produce many small electrical currents called instantaneous vectors.

- The mean, or average, of all the instantaneous vectors is called the mean vector.

- When an impulse is traveling toward a positive electrode, the ECG machine records it as a positive or upward deflection.

- When the impulse is traveling away from a positive electrode and toward a negative electrode, the ECG machine records it as a negative or downward deflection.

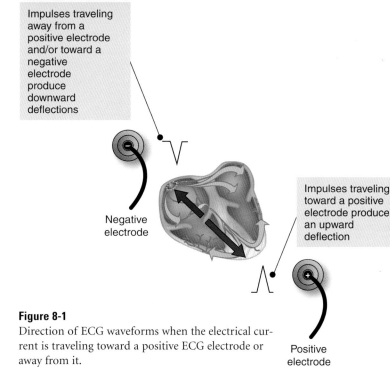

Impulses traveling away from a positive electrode and/or toward a negative electrode produce downward deflections

Negative electrode

Impulses traveling toward a positive electrode produce an upward deflection

Positive electrode

Figure 8-1
Direction of ECG waveforms when the electrical current is traveling toward a positive ECG electrode or away from it.

Mean QRS Vector

- The sum of all the small vectors of ventricular depolarization is called the mean QRS vector.

- Because the depolarization vectors of the thicker left ventricle are larger, the mean QRS axis points downward and toward the patient's left side.

- Changes in the size or condition of the heart muscle and/or conduction system can affect the direction of the mean QRS vector.

- If an area of the heart is enlarged or damaged, specific ECG leads can provide a view of that portion of the heart.

- While there are several methods used to determine the direction of the patient's electrical axis, the easiest is the four-quadrant method.

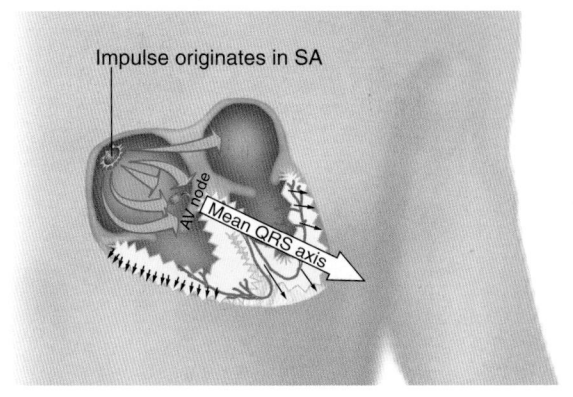

Figure 8-2
Direction of of the mean QRS axis.

Method for determining QRS axis

- The four-quadrant method works in the following manner:
  - An imaginary circle is drawn over the patient's chest; it represents the frontal plane.
  - Within the circle are six bisecting lines, each representing one of the six limb leads.
  - The intersection of all lines divides the circle into equal, 30-degree segments.
- The mean QRS axis normally remains between 0 and +90° degrees.
  - As long as it stays in this range it is considered normal.
  - If it is outside this range, it is considered abnormal.
  - Leads I and aV$_F$ can be used to determine if the mean QRS is in its normal position.

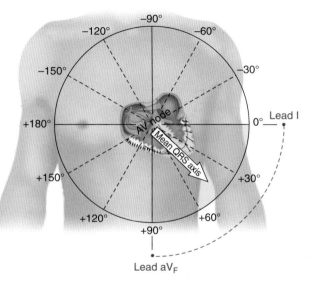

Figure 8-3
Normal direction of the mean QRS axis.

Lead I

- Lead I is oriented at 0° (located at the three o'clock position).

- A positive QRS complex indicates the mean QRS axis is moving from right to left in a normal manner and directed somewhere between −90° and +90° (the right half of the circle).

- If the QRS complex points down (negative), then the impulses are moving from left to right; this is considered abnormal.

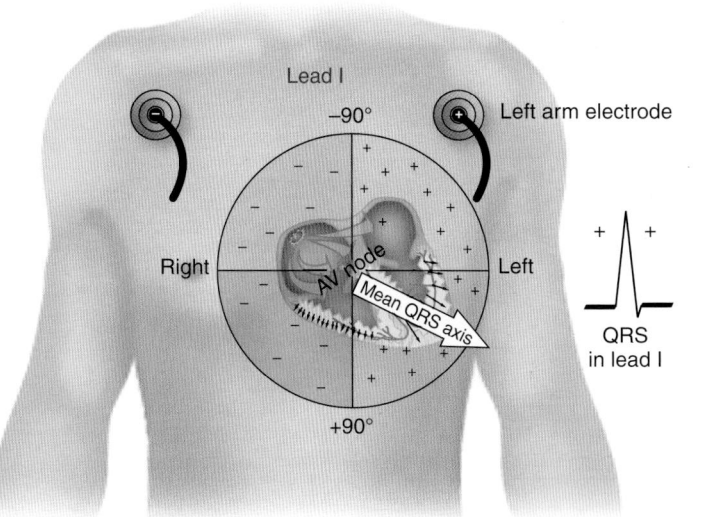

Figure 8-4
A positive QRS complex is seen in lead I if the mean QRS axis is directed anywhere between −90 and +90.

Lead aV$_F$

- Lead aV$_F$ is oriented at +90° and is located at the six o'clock position.

- If the mean QRS axis is directed anywhere between 0° and −180° (the bottom half of the circle), you can expect aV$_F$ lead to record a positive QRS complex.

- If the mean QRS is directed toward the top half of the circle, the QRS complex points downward.

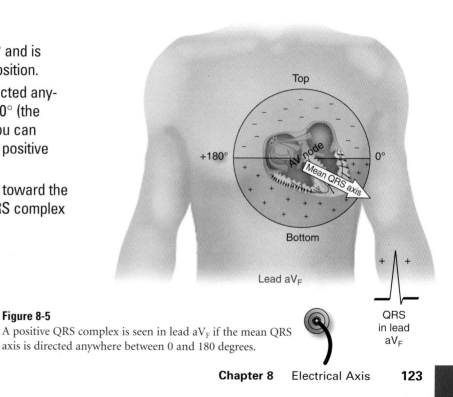

Figure 8-5

A positive QRS complex is seen in lead aV$_F$ if the mean QRS axis is directed anywhere between 0 and 180 degrees.

Axis deviation

- Positive QRS complexes in lead I and aV$_F$ indicate a normal QRS axis.

- A negative QRS complex in lead I and an upright QRS complex in lead aV$_F$ indicates right axis deviation.

- An upright QRS complex in lead I and a negative QRS complex in lead aV$_F$ indicates left axis deviation.

- Negative QRS complexes in both lead I and lead aV$_F$ indicates extreme axis deviation.

- Persons who are thin, obese, or pregnant can have axis deviation due to a shift in the position of the apex of the heart.

- Myocardial infarction, enlargement, or hypertrophy of one or both of the heart's chambers, and hemiblock can also cause axis deviation.

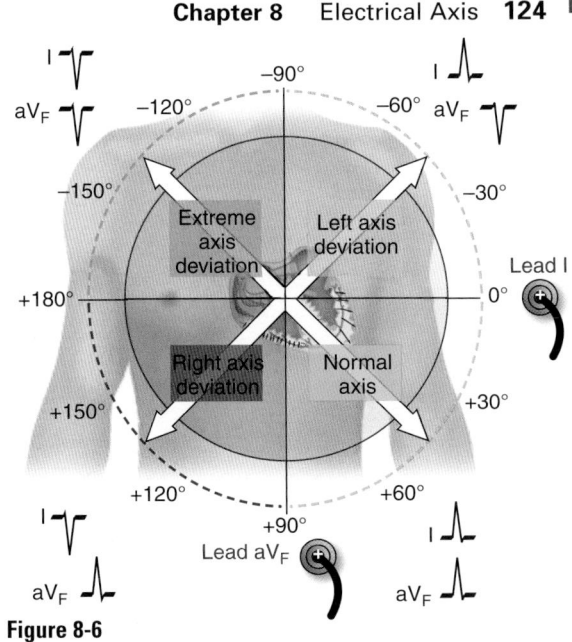

Figure 8-6

Direction of QRS complexes in lead I and aV$_F$ indicate changes in size or condition of the heart muscle and/or conduction system.

Hypertrophy, Bundle Branch Block, and Preexcitation

9

What is in this chapter

- Right atrial enlargement
- Right ventricular hypertrophy
- Right bundle branch block
- Left atrial enlargement
- Left ventricular hypertrophy
- Left bundle branch block
- Left anterior hemiblock
- Left posterior hemiblock
- Wolff-Parkinson-White (WPW) syndrome
- Lown-Ganong-Levine (LGL) syndrome

Right atrial enlargement

- Leads II and V_1 provide the necessary information to assess atrial enlargement.
- Indicators of right atrial enlargement include:
  - An increase in the amplitude of the first part of the P wave.
  - The P wave is taller than 2.5 mm.
  - If the P wave is biphasic, the initial component is taller than the terminal component.
- The width of the P wave, however, stays within normal limits because its terminal part originates from the left atria, which depolarizes normally if left atrial enlargement is absent.

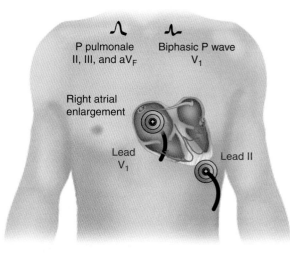

Figure 9-1
Right atrial enlargement leads to an increase in the amplitude of the first part of the P wave.

Left atrial enlargement

- Indicators of left atrial enlargement include:
  - The amplitude of the terminal portion of the P wave may increase in V_1.
  - The terminal (left atrial) portion of the P wave drops at least 1 mm below the iso-electric line (in lead V_1).
  - There is an increase in the duration or width of the terminal portion of the P wave of at least one small square (0.04 seconds).
- Often the presence of ECG evidence of left atrial enlargement only reflects a nonspecific conduction irregularity. However, it may also be the result of mitral valve stenosis causing the left atria to enlarge to force blood across the stenotic (tight) mitral valve.

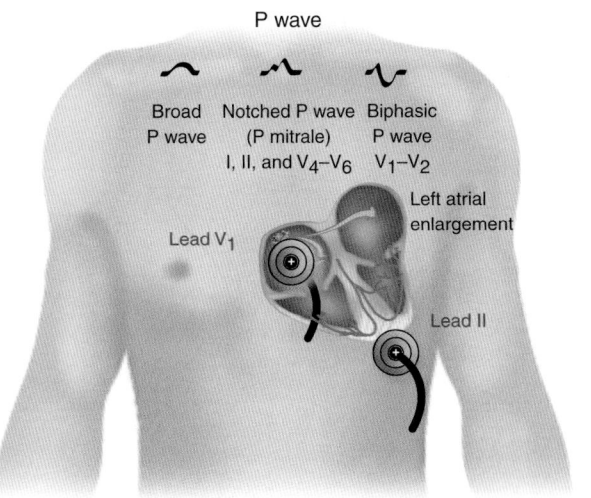

Figure 9-2
Left atrial enlargement leads to an increase in the amplitude and width of the terminal part of the P wave.

Right ventricular hypertrophy

- Key indicators of right ventricular hypertrophy include:
  - The presence of right axis deviation (with the QRS axis exceeding +100°).
- The R wave larger than the S wave in lead V_1, whereas the S wave is larger than the R wave in lead V_6.

Left ventricular hypertrophy

- Key ECG indicators of left ventricular hypertrophy include:
  - Increased R wave amplitude in those leads overlying the left ventricle.
  - The S waves are smaller in leads overlying the left ventricle, but larger in leads overlying the right ventricle.

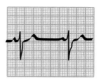
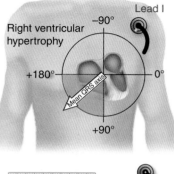
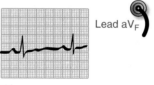

aV_F

Figure 9-3

In right ventricular hypertrophy the QRS axis moves to between +90 and +180 degrees. The QRS complexes in right ventricular hypertrophy are slightly more negative in lead I and positive in lead aV_F.

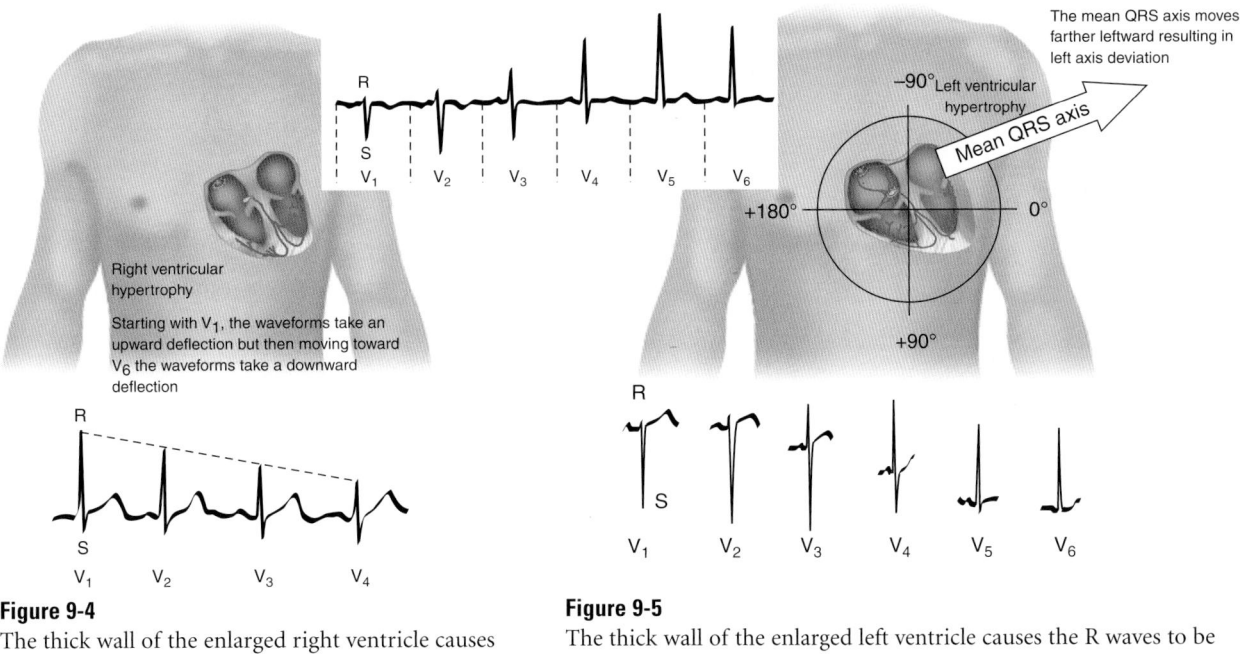

Figure 9-4

The thick wall of the enlarged right ventricle causes the R waves to be more positive in the leads that lie closer to lead V_1.

Figure 9-5

The thick wall of the enlarged left ventricle causes the R waves to be more positive in the leads that lie closer to lead V_6 and the S waves to be larger in the leads closer to V_1.

Right bundle branch block

- The best leads for identifying right bundle branch are V_1 and V_2.
- Right bundle block causes the QRS complex to have a unique shape — its appearance has been likened to rabbit ears or the letter "M."
  - As the left ventricle depolarizes, it produces the initial R and S waves, but as the right ventricle begins its delayed depolarization, it produces a tall R wave (called the R').
- In the left lateral leads overlying the left ventricle (I, aV_L, V_5, and V_6), late right ventricular depolarization causes reciprocal late broad S waves to be generated.

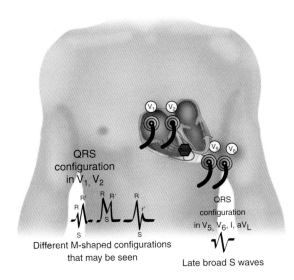

QRS configuration in V_1, V_2

Different M-shaped configurations that may be seen

QRS configuration in V_5, V_6, I, aV_L

Late broad S waves

Figure 9-6
In right bundle branch block, conduction through the right bundle is blocked causing depolarization of the right ventricle to be delayed; it does not start until the left ventricle is almost fully depolarized.

Left bundle branch block

- Leads V_5 and V_6 are best for identifying left bundle branch block.
  - QRS complexes in these leads normally have tall R waves, whereas delayed left ventricular depolarization leads to a marked prolongation in the rise of those tall R waves, which will either be flattened on top or notched (with two tiny points), referred to as an R, R' wave.
  - True rabbit ears are less likely to be seen than in right bundle branch block.
- Leads V_1 and V_2 (leads overlying the right ventricle) will show reciprocal, broad, deep S waves.

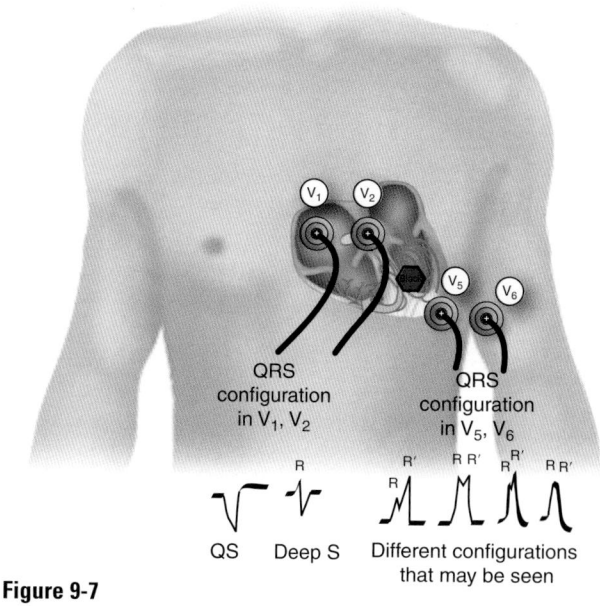

Figure 9-7

In left bundle branch block, conduction through the left bundle is blocked causing depolarization of the left ventricle to be delayed; it does not start until the right ventricle is almost fully depolarized.

Left anterior hemiblock

- With left anterior hemiblock, depolarization of the left ventricle occurs progressing in an inferior-to-superior and right-to-left direction.

  - This causes the axis of ventricular depolarization to be redirected upward and slightly to the left, producing tall positive R waves in the left lateral leads and deep S waves inferiorly.

  - This results in left axis deviation with an upright QRS complex in lead I and a negative QRS in lead aV$_F$.

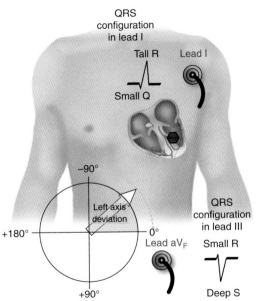

Figure 9-8

With left anterior hemiblock, conduction down the left anterior fascicle is blocked resulting in all the current rushing down the left posterior fascicle to the inferior surface of the heart.

Left posterior hemiblock

- In left posterior hemiblock, ventricular myocardial depolarization occurs in a superior-to-inferior and left-to-right direction.

  - This causes the main electrical axis to be directed downward and to the right, producing tall R waves inferiorly and deep S waves in the left lateral leads.

  - This results in right axis deviation. With a negative QRS in lead I and a positive QRS in lead aV$_F$.

- In contrast to complete left and right bundle branch block, in hemiblocks, the QRS complex is not prolonged.

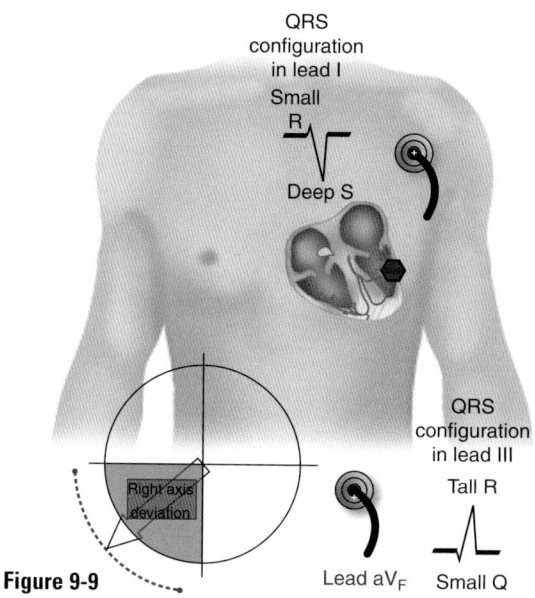

Figure 9-9
With left posterior hemiblock, conduction down the left posterior fascicle is blocked resulting in all the current rushing down the left anterior fascicle to the myocardium.

Wolff-Parkinson-White (WPW) syndrome

- WPW is identified through the following ECG features:
  - Rhythm is regular.
  - P waves are normal.
  - QRS complexes are widened due to a characteristic slurred initial upstroke, called the delta wave.
  - PR interval is usually shortened (less than 0.12 seconds).
- WPW can predispose the patient to various tachydysrhythmias; the most common is PSVT.

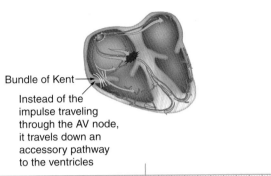

Bundle of Kent—

Instead of the impulse traveling through the AV node, it travels down an accessory pathway to the ventricles

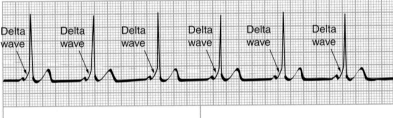

Delta wave · Delta wave · Delta wave · Delta wave · Delta wave · Delta wave

Figure 9-10
In WPW, the bundle of Kent, an accessory pathway, connects the atrium to the ventricles, bypassing the AV node. The QRS complex is widened due to premature activation of the ventricles.

Lown-Ganong-Levine (LGL) syndrome

- LGL is identified through the following ECG features:
- Rhythm is regular.
  - P waves are normal.
  - The PR interval is less than 0.12 seconds.
  - The QRS complex is not widened.
  - There is no delta wave.
- WPW and LGL are called preexcitation syndromes and are the result of accessory conduction pathways between the atria and ventricles.

Impulse travels down through the atria

James fibers

Instead of traveling through the AV node, the impulse is carried to the ventricles by way of an intranodal accessory pathway

Figure 9-11

In LGL, the impulse travels through an intranodal accessory pathway, referred to as the James fibers, bypassing the normal delay within the AV node. This produces a shortening of the PR interval but no widening of the QRS complex.

Myocardial Ischemia and Infarction

What is in this chapter

- ECG changes associated with ischemia, injury, and infarction
- Identifying the location of myocardial ischemia, injury, and infarction
  - Anterior
  - Septal
  - Lateral
  - Inferior
  - Posterior

ECG changes associated with ischemia, injury, and infarction

- The ECG can help identify the presence of ischemia, injury, and/or infarction of the heart muscle.
- The three key ECG indicators are:
  - Changes in the T wave (peaking or inversion).
  - Changes in the ST segment (depression or elevation).
  - Enlarged Q waves or appearance of new Q waves.
- ST segment elevation is the earliest reliable sign that myocardial infarction has occurred and tells us the myocardial infarction is acute.
- Pathologic Q waves indicate the presence of irreversible myocardial damage or past myocardial infarction.
- Myocardial infarction can occur without the development of Q waves.

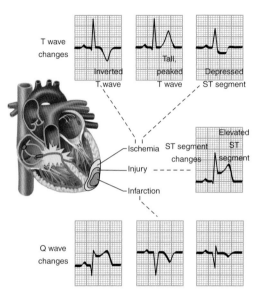

Figure 10-1
Key ECG changes with ischemia, injury, or infarction

Identifying the location of myocardial ischemia, injury, and infarction

- Leads V_1, V_2, V_3, and V_4 provide the best view for identifying anterior myocardial infarction.

- Leads V_1, V_2, and V_3 overlie the ventricular septum, so ischemic changes seen in these leads, and possibly in the adjacent precordial leads, are often considered to be septal infarctions.

- Lateral infarction is identified by ECG changes such as ST segment elevation; T wave inversion; and the development of significant Q waves in leads I, aV_L, V_5, and V_6.

- Inferior infarction is determined by ECG changes such as ST segment elevation; T wave inversion; and the development of significant Q waves in leads II, III, and aV_F.

- Posterior infarctions can be diagnosed by looking for reciprocal changes in leads V_1 and V_2.

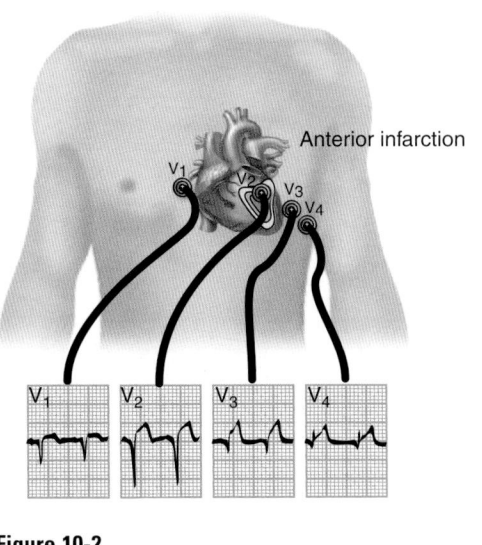

Figure 10-2
Leads V_1, V_2, V_3, and V_4 are used to identify anterior myocardial infarction.

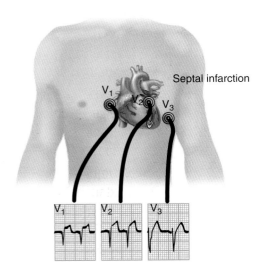

Figure 10-3
Leads V_1, V_2, and V_3 are used to identify septal myocardial infarction.

Septal infarction

Figure 10-4
Leads I, aV_L, V_5, and V_6 are used to identify lateral myocardial infarction.

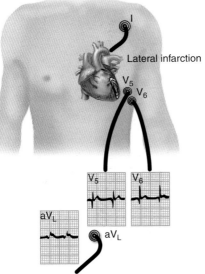

Lateral infarction

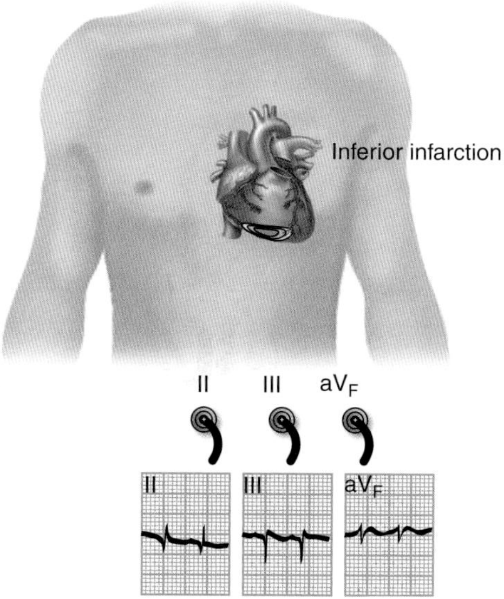

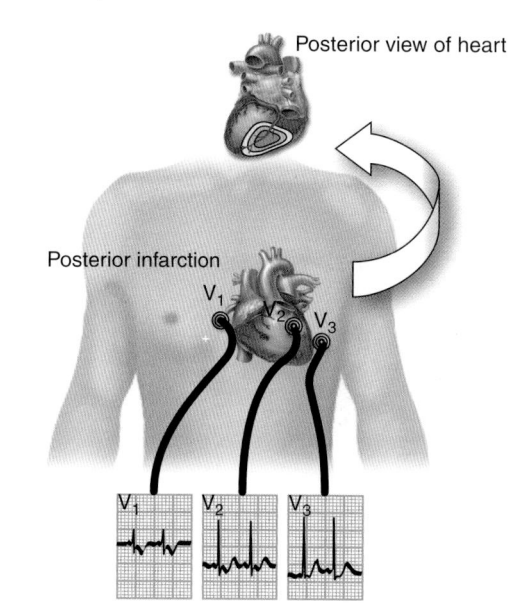

Figure 10-5

Leads II, III, and aV$_F$ are used to identify inferior myocardial infarction.

Figure 10-6

Leads V$_1$ and V$_2$ are used to identify posterior myocardial infarction.

Other Cardiac Conditions

11

What is in this chapter

- Pericarditis
- Pericardial effusion with low-voltage QRS complexes
- Pericardial effusion with electrical alternans
- Pulmonary embolism
- Pacemakers
- Electrolyte imbalances
- Digoxin effects seen on the ECG

Pericarditis

- Initially with pericarditis the T wave is upright and may be elevated. During the recovery phase it inverts.

- The ST segment is elevated and usually flat or concave.

- While the signs and symptoms of pericarditis and myocardial infarction are similar, certain features of the ECG can be helpful in differentiating between the two:

  - The ST segment and T wave changes in pericarditis are diffuse resulting in ECG changes being present in all leads.

  - In pericarditis, T wave inversion usually occurs only after the ST segments have returned to base line. In myocardial infarction, T wave inversion is usually seen before ST segment normalization. (continued)

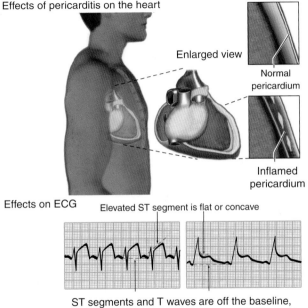

Effects of pericarditis on the heart

Enlarged view

Normal pericardium

Inflamed pericardium

Effects on ECG   Elevated ST segment is flat or concave

ST segments and T waves are off the baseline, gradually angling back down to the next QRS complex

Figure 11-1

Pericarditis and ST segment elevation.

   ○ In pericarditis, Q wave development does not occur.

Pericardial effusion with low-voltage QRS complexes

- Pericardial effusion is a buildup of an abnormal amount of fluid and/or a change in the character of the fluid in the pericardial space.

   ○ The pericardial space is the space between the heart and the pericardial sac.

- Formation of a substantial pericardial effusion dampens the electrical output of the heart, resulting in low-voltage QRS complex in all leads.

- However, the ST segment and T wave changes of pericarditis may still be seen.

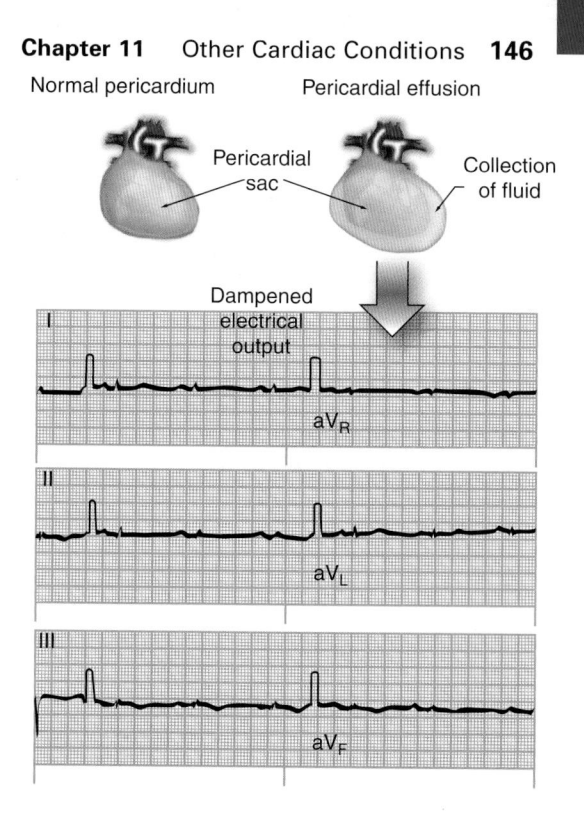

Figure 11-2
Pericardial effusion with low-voltage QRS complexes.

Pericardial effusion with electrical alternans

- If a pericardial effusion is large enough, the heart may rotate freely within the fluid-filled sac.

- This can cause electrical alternans, a condition in which the electrical axis of the heart varies with each beat.

- A varying axis is most easily recognized on the ECG by the presence of QRS complexes that change in height with each successive beat.

- This condition can also affect the P and T waves.

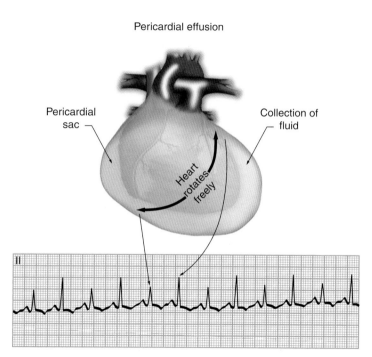

Figure 11-3 Pericardial effusion with electrical alternans.

Pulmonary embolism

- ECG changes that suggest the development of a massive pulmonary embolus include:
  - Tall, symmetrically peaked P waves in leads II, III, and aV_F and sharply peaked biphasic P waves in leads V_1 and V_2.
  - A large S wave in lead I, a deep Q wave in lead III, and an inverted T wave in lead III. This is called the $S_1 Q_3 T_3$ pattern.
  - ST segment depression in lead II.
  - Right bundle branch block (usually subsides after the patient improves).
  - The QRS axis is greater than $+90°$ (right axis deviation).
  - The T waves are inverted in leads V_1–V_4.
  - Q waves are generally limited to lead III.

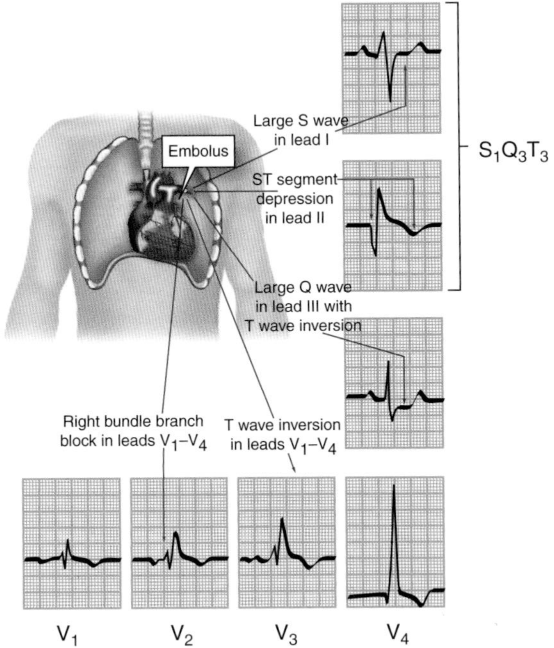

Embolus

Large S wave in lead I

ST segment depression in lead II

Large Q wave in lead III with T wave inversion

$S_1 Q_3 T_3$

Right bundle branch block in leads V_1–V_4

T wave inversion in leads V_1–V_4

V_1 V_2 V_3 V_4

Figure 11-4
ECG changes seen with pulmonary embolism.

Pacemakers

- A pacemaker is an artificial device that produces an impulse from a power source and conveys it to the myocardium.

- It provides an electrical stimulus for hearts whose intrinsic ability to generate an impulse or whose ability to conduct electrical current is impaired.

- The power source is generally positioned subcutaneously, and the electrodes are threaded to the right atrium and right ventricle through veins that drain to the heart.

- The impulse flows throughout the heart causing the muscle to depolarize and initiate a contraction.

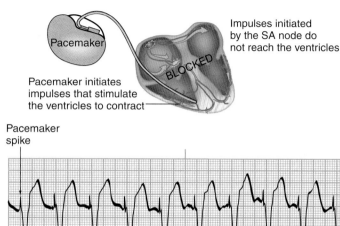

Pacemaker initiates impulses that stimulate the ventricles to contract

Impulses initiated by the SA node do not reach the ventricles

BLOCKED

Pacemaker spike

Figure 11-5
Pacemakers are used to provide electrical stimuli for hearts with an impaired ability to conduct an electrical impulse.

Pacemaker impulses

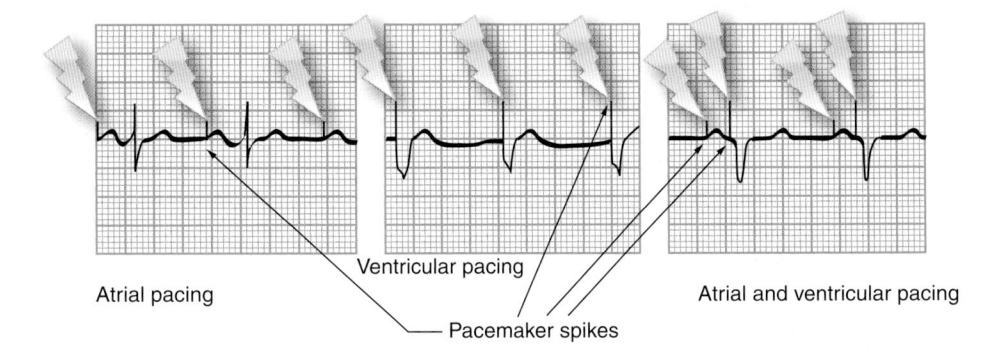

Figure 11-6
Location of pacemaker spikes on the ECG tracing with each type of pacemaker.

Ventricular pacing

Atrial pacing

Pacemaker spikes

Atrial and ventricular pacing

- An atrial pacemaker will produce a spike trailed by a P wave and a normal QRS complex.
- With an AV sequential pacemaker, two spikes are seen, one that precedes a P wave and one that precedes a wide, bizarre QRS complex.
- With a ventricular pacemaker, the resulting QRS complex is wide and bizarre. Because the electrodes are positioned in the right ventricle, the right ventricle will contract first, then the left ventricle. This produces a pattern identical to left bundle branch block, with delayed left ventricular depolarization.

Electrolyte imbalances

Hypokalemia

- ECG changes seen with serious hypokalemia include:
  - ST segment depression.
  - Flattening of the T wave.
  - Appearance of U waves.
  - Prolongation of the QT interval.

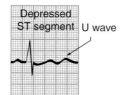

T wave flattens (or is inverted) and U wave appears

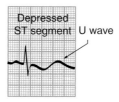

U wave becomes more prominent

Figure 11-7
ECG effects seen with hypokalemia.

Figure 11-8
ECG effects seen with hyperkalemia.

Hyperkalemia

- ECG changes seen with hyperkalemia include:
  - Peaked T waves (tenting).
  - Flattened P waves.
  - Prolonged PR interval (1st-degree AV heart block).
  - Widened QRS complex.
  - Deepened S waves and merging of S and T waves.
  - Concave up and down slope of the T wave.
  - Sine-wave pattern.

Peaked, narrow T waves in all leads

T wave peaking increases, P waves flatten and QRS complexes widen

Widened QRS complexes and peaked T waves become almost indistinguishable, forming what are described as a "sine-wave pattern"

Hypercalcemia/ Hypocalcemia

- Alterations in serum calcium levels mainly affect the QT interval.
- Hypocalcemia prolongs the QT interval while hypercalcemia shortens it.
- Torsades de pointes, a variant of ventricular tachycardia, is seen in patients with prolonged QT intervals.

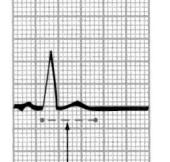

Short QT interval

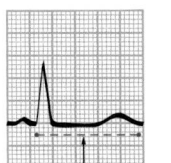

Prolonged QT interval

Figure 11-9
ECG effects seen with hypocalcemia and hypercalcemia.

Digoxin effects seen on the ECG

- Digoxin produces a characteristic gradual downward curve of the ST segment (it looks like a ladle).
  - The R wave slurs into the ST segment.
  - Sometimes the T wave is lost in this scooping effect. The lowest portion of the ST segment is depressed below the baseline.
- When seen, the T waves have shorter amplitude and can be biphasic.
- The QT interval is usually shorter than anticipated, and the U waves are more visible. Also, the PR interval may be prolonged.

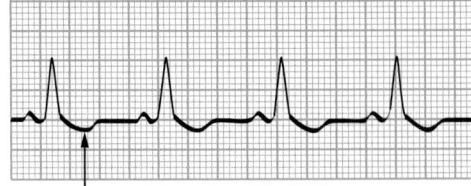

Gradual downward curve of the ST segment

Figure 11-10
Effects of digoxin on the ECG.

Index